LONG LIVE REVOLUTION!

LONG LIVE REVOLUTION!
ESSAYS AND OTHER WORKS

BHAGAT SINGH

Foreword by
Chaman Lal

JAICO PUBLISHING HOUSE
Ahmedabad Bangalore Chennai
Delhi Hyderabad Kolkata Mumbai

Published by Jaico Publishing House
A-2 Jash Chambers, 7-A Sir Phirozshah Mehta Road
Fort, Mumbai - 400 001
jaicopub@jaicobooks.com
www.jaicobooks.com

© Jaico Publishing House

LONG LIVE REVOLUTION!
ESSAYS AND OTHER WORKS OF BHAGAT SINGH
ISBN 978-81-19792-64-1

First Jaico Impression: 2024

No part of this book may be reproduced or utilized in
any form or by any means, electronic or
mechanical including photocopying, recording or by any
information storage and retrieval system,
without permission in writing from the publishers.

Page design and layout by
Special Effects Graphics Design Company, Mumbai

Contents

Foreword   vii

1. "My Life Has Been Dedicated to the Cause of Azad-E-Hind"   1
2. "Blood Sprinkled on the Day of Holi, Babbar Akalis on the Crucifix!"   5
3. Religious Riots and Their Solution   15
4. Religion and Our Freedom Struggle   23
5. The Issue of Untouchability   31
6. Satyagraha and Strikes   41
7. Students and Politics   49
8. New Leaders and Their Different Ideas   55
9. What Is Anarchism – I, II, and III   65
10. 'Beware, Ye Tyrants; Beware'   85
11. "It Takes a Loud Voice to Make the Deaf Hear!"   89
12. "Do Away with the Fear of Doing Radical Things"   95
13. Joint Statement: Full Text of Statement of Bhagat Singh and B.K. Dutt Regarding the Assembly Bomb Case   101
14. Hunger-Strikers' Demand   113

15	Message to Punjab Students' Conference	117
16	On the Slogan of 'Long Live Revolution!'	121
17	Why I Am an Atheist	127
18	"Show the World That the Revolutionaries Not Only Die for Their Ideals but Can Face Every Calamity!"	149
19	"I Want to Tell You That Obstacles Make a Man Perfect"	153
20	Hunger-Strikers' Demands Reiterated	163
21	"I Feel as Though I Have Been Stabbed in the Back"	175
22	To Young Political Workers	181
23	"We Are War Prisoners, Shoot Us, Do Not Hang Us!"	215
24	"Mr. Kishan's Action Was Part of the Struggle Itself"	221
25	Introduction to Dreamland	229
26	Manifestos of Naujawan Bharat Sabha and Hindustan Socialist Republican Association	237
Sources		253

Foreword

Bhagat Singh (September 28, 1907 – March 23, 1931) holds the title of *Shaheed-e-Azam* 'The Supreme Martyr' in the truest sense. It's a badge of honour rightfully bestowed upon him by the Indian people, for inspiring the masses and fellow revolutionaries through his contributions, and for readily walking to the gallows for India's freedom. With his towering intellect and immense popularity, Bhagat Singh—at merely 23 years of age—managed to intimidate the British Empire during his short political life of a little over seven years, through his uncompromising struggle against colonialism and imperialism. His legacy continues to thrive and remain relevant over the century through his speeches and writings, which have been reproduced by numerous publications in several Indian languages.

Born into a family of freedom fighters, Bhagat Singh shared the revolutionary traits and fierce patriotism of his father Kishan Singh and uncles Ajit Singh and Swarn Singh. His inclination towards the communist movement inspired his political ideas and actions. He read books that were primarily on Marxism, politics, economics, history, and literature. It is not without reason that eminent historian Bipan Chandra wrote in an introduction to Bhagat Singh's widely-read essay *'Why I am an Atheist'* in the 1970s: "During 1925 to 1928, Bhagat Singh read voraciously, devouring in particular books on the Russian revolution and the Soviet Union, even though getting hold of such books was in itself at the time a revolutionary and difficult task. He also tried to inculcate the reading and thinking habit among his fellow revolutionaries and younger comrades."

Bhagat Singh is widely known for his patriotism and courage. However, I would like to call attention to his organized thinking which is reflected in his writings and speeches. The last years of his life (from December 1928 to March 1931), which he spent in Lahore jail for killing assistant superintendent of police John Saunders, was the time when he read and wrote voraciously, despite being certain that he is going to be executed for his political actions. Bhagat Singh was famously known to have been reading *Reminiscences of Lenin* and studying the life of Lenin minutes before he was being taken to the gallows. Praising this aspect of Bhagat Singh, Punjabi revolutionary poet Pash (Avtar Singh Sandhu), who was murdered by Khalistani terrorists on March 23, 1988, had said in one of his prose pieces: "Indian youth have to read the next page of Lenin's book, left unread by Bhagat Singh at his death". It is, therefore, crucial to understand that Bhagat Singh was a profound thinker, a fierce revolutionary, and a prolific writer for a man of his years.

Bhagat Singh's writing journey began in 1923 when he was 16 years old, and around the same time, he joined the revolutionary movement by being a member of the newly-organized Hindustan Republican Association (later came to be known as Hindustan Socialist Republican Association-HSRA). One could call him a polyglot as he had good command over Urdu, English, Hindi, and Punjabi, and was also known to have been well-versed in Sanskrit and Bengali. He was also learning Persian in jail. The essays and letters selected in this book—most were originally written in English, while some were in Hindi, Punjabi and Urdu—provide you with an insight into his thought process as a revolutionary, thinker, and writer.

In 1923, a concerned grandmother began scouting brides for a 16-year-old Bhagat Singh who was then studying in National College, Lahore. The teenager then wrote to his father, Kishan Singh, that his "life has been dedicated to the cause of *Azad-e-Hind* (freedom of India)" and that there is no place for worldly pleasures or comfort in his life. This letter (Refer to Page 1), which was originally written in Urdu, exhibited his immense clarity of thought and passion towards his nation's freedom struggle. He then went on to become a part of the editorial staff of the Hindi newspaper, *Pratap*, where he met other revolutionaries like Batukeshwar Dutt, Shiv Verma, and Bejoy Kumar Sinha.

One of the remarkable revolutionary acts by Bhagat Singh, along with his HSRA comrade Batukeshwar Dutt, that left an indelible impression on the masses was throwing non-lethal bombs in the Central Assembly, Delhi, during the enactment of Public Safety and Trade Disputes Bills by the British colonial government on April 8, 1929. With the slogans of '*Inquilab Zindabad!* (Long Live Revolution!)' and 'Down with Imperialism!' reverberating in the assembly hall, the two revolutionaries threw non-lethal bombs to "make the deaf hear" (Refer to page 89). The phrase '*Inquilab Zindabad!*' was coined by Moulana Hasrat Mohani, the Indian freedom fighter, Islamic scholar, and noted Urdu poet, in 1921. However, it was immortalized by Bhagat Singh and his fellow HSRA comrades who adopted the revolutionary cry as their official slogan.

In his short political career spanning a little over seven years (from 1923 to 1931), Bhagat Singh rigorously documented his thoughts and ideas on paper (presuming he may not live long) so that they don't get misconstrued. The political letters from the jail to his comrades, young political workers, and statements are a part of the popular public discourse. They have been reproduced and translated in several languages. However, this compilation also includes crucial essays (Refer to Pages 15-65) he wrote while he was working with the Punjabi journal *Kirti*. The essays—*'The Religious Riots and Their Solution'*, *'Religion and Our Freedom Struggle'*, *'The Issue Of Untouchability'*, *'Satyagraha and Strikes'*, *'Students and Politics'*, *'New Leaders and their Different Ideas'*, and *'What is Anarchism—I, II, and III'*—bear testimony to the fact that Bhagat Singh made best use of the power of his pen to express his thoughts on a wide range of topics like religion, caste, anarchism, and so on, through these editorials. These essays have been sourced from my book *Shahid Bhagat Singh Dastavejo Ke Aaine Mein* (A Hindi collection published by Publications Division, Ministry of Information and Broadcasting, Government of India) edited by me and translated in English by Dr. Hina Nandrajog, Officiating Principal, Vivekananda College at the University of Delhi.

It may not be possible to quantify Bhagat Singh's contribution as an ideologue, however, he certainly managed to provoke fiery patriotic values in millions of young minds of his time through his words. But he was not alone in this; he had unwavering support of his comrades at the Naujawan Bharat Sabha (NBS) and Hindustan Socialist Republican

Association (HSRA). The manifestos of NBS and HSRA (Refer page 237)—drafted by Bhagwati Charan Vohra (founder-propaganda-secretary of NBS) in consultation with Bhagat Singh—provide great insights into the political ideals of these revolutionaries.

It is difficult to encapsulate Bhagat Singh's brand of revolutionary movement in a few pages, however, it is crucial that we understand the great revolutionary's ideas on socialism, Marxism, religion, caste, and politics through his writings presented in this book. The idea and spirit of Bhagat Singh have been immortalized in the pages of Indian history; I hope that they continue to thrive and remain relevant to the youth today.

— **Chaman Lal (Retd. Professor, JNU)**

> Honorary Adviser at Bhagat Singh Archives and Resource Centre, Department of Delhi Archives, Government of NCT of Delhi

1

"My Life Has Been Dedicated to the Cause of Azad-E-Hind"
A 16-year-old Bhagat Singh Wrote to His father
(1923)

When a 16-year-old Bhagat Singh's grandmother began scouting brides for him, he was still a student at the National College, Lahore. Seeing his counter-argument not working with his grandmother, he wrote to his father, Kishan Singh, stating his "life has been dedicated to the noblest cause of *Azad-e-Hind*" and that worldly pleasures or comfort held no attraction for him. This letter, which was originally written in Urdu, exhibited his immense clarity of thought and passion towards contributing to his nation's freedom struggle. He then went on to edit the Hindi weekly newspaper—*Pratap*—where he met other revolutionaries like Batukeshwar Dutt, Shiv Verma, and Bejoy Kumar Sinha.

Respected Father,

Namaste.

My life has been dedicated to the cause of *Azad-e-Hind*. Therefore, there is no place for comfort and worldly pleasures in my life.

You would remember that when I was young, Bapu Ji had announced during my *yajnopavit* (thread) ceremony that I would be dedicated to serve the homeland. Hence, I am fulfilling the promise taken at that time.

I hope you will forgive me.

Yours obediently,
Bhagat Singh

2

"Blood Sprinkled on the Day of Holi, Babbar Akalis on the Crucifix!"
Bhagat Singh on martyrs of Babbar Akali movement
(March, 1926)

In 1925-26, Bhagat Singh was at Kanpur, working under Ganesh Shankar Vidharthi in the Hindi weekly newspaper *Pratap*. While at Kanpur, he wrote this article about the martyrs of Babbar Akali movement and signed it as *"Ek Punjabi Yuvak"* (a Punjabi youth). It was published in *Pratap* on March 15, 1926.

On the day of Holi, February 27, 1926, when we were getting high on our enjoyment, a terrible thing was happening in a corner of this great province. When you will hear it, you will shudder! You will tremble! On that day, six brave Babbar Akalis were hanged in the Lahore Central Jail. Shri kishan Singhji Gadagajja, Shri Santa Singhji, Shri Dilip Sinhghji, Shri Nand Singhji, Shri Karam Singhji and Shri Dharam Singhji, had been showing a great indifference to the trial for the last two years, which speaks of their fond waiting for this day. After months, the judge gave his verdict. Five to be hanged, many for life imprisonment or exile, and sentences of very long imprisonments. The accused heroes thundered. Even the skies echoed with their triumphant slogans. Then an appeal was preferred. Instead of five, now six were sent to the noose. The same day the news came that a mercy petition was sent. The Punjab Secretary declared that the hanging would be put off. We were waiting but, all of a sudden, on the very day of Holi, we saw a small contingent of mourners carrying the dead bodies of the heroes towards the cremation site. Then last rites were completed quietly.

The city was still celebrating. Colour was still being thrown on the passers-by. What a terrible indifference! If they were misguided, if they were frenzied, let them be so. They were fearless patriots, in any case. Whatever they did, they did it for this wretched country. They could not bear injustice. They could not countenance the fallen nation. The oppression on the poor people became insufferable for them. They could not tolerate exploitation of the masses, they challenged and jumped into action. They were full of life. Oh! the terrible toll of their dedicated deeds! You are blessed! After the death, friends and foes are all alike—this is the ideal of men. Even if they might have done something hateful, their lives at the altar of our nation, is something to the opposite side, could highly and uninhibitedly appreciate the courage, patriotism and commitment of the brave revolutionary of Bengal, Jatin Mukherjee, while mourning his death. But we the cowards and human wretches lack the courage of even sighing and putting off our celebrations even for a moment. What a disheartening deed! The poor! they were given "adequate" punishment even by the standards of the brutal bureaucrats. An act of a terrible tragedy thus ended, but the curtain is not down as yet. The drama will have some more terrible scenes. The story is quite lengthy; we have to turn back a little to know about it.

The non-cooperation movement was at its peak. The Punjab did not lag behind. The Sikhs also rose from their deep slumber and it was quite an awakening. The Akali Movement had started. Sacrifices were made in abundance. Master Mota Singh, ex-teacher of Khalsa Middle School, Mahalpur (district Hoshiarpur), delivered a speech. A warrant was issued against him, but the idea of availing the hospitality of the crown did not find his favour. He was against offering arrest to fill the jails. His speeches still continued. In Kot-Phatuhi village, a big *'deevan'* was called. Police cordoned the area off from all sides; even then Master Mota Singh delivered his speech. The whole audience stood up and dispersed on the orders of the persident of the meeting. The Master escaped mysteriously. This hide-and-seek continued for long. The government was in a frenzy. At last, a friend turned traitor, and Master Saheb was arrested after a year and a half. This was the first scene of that horrible drama.

The *"Guru ka bagh"* movement was started. The hired hoodlums were there to attack the unarmed heroes and to beat them half-dead. Could anyone who looked at or listened to this, help being mover? It was a case of arrests and arrests everywhere. A warrant was also issued against Sardar Kishan Singhji Gadagajja, but he also belonged to the same category and did not offer arrest. The police strained all its nerves but he always escaped. He had an organization of his own. He could not bear the violence against unarmed agitators. He felt the need of using arms along with this peaceful movement.

On the one hand, the dogs, the hunting dogs of the government, were searching for the clues, to get his scent; on the other, it was decided to "reform" the sycophants (Jholi Chukkas). Sardar Kishan Singhji used to say that we must keep ourselves armed for our own security, but we should not take any precipitate action for the time being. The majority was against this. At last, it was decided that three of them should give their names, take all the blame on themselves and start reforming these sycophants. Sardar Karam Singhji, Sardar Dhanna Singhji and Sardar Uday Singhji stepped forward. Just keep aside the question of its propriety for a moment and imagine the scene when they took the oath:

We will sacrifice our all in the service of the country. We swear to die fighting but not to go to the prison.

What a beautiful, sanctified scene it must have been, when these people who had given up all of their family affections, were taking such an oath! Where is the end of sacrifice? Where is the limit to courage and fearlessness? Where does the extremity of idealism reside?

Near a station on Shyam Churasi-Hoshiarpur railway branch line, a Subedar became the first victim. After that, all these three declared their names. The government tried its best to arrest them, but failed. Sardar Kishan Singh Gadagajja was once almost trapped by the police near Roorki Kalan. A young man who accompanied him, fell down after getting injured, and was captured. But even there, Kishan Singhji escaped with the help of his arms. He met a Sadhu on the way who told him about a herb in his possession which could materialise all his plans and work miracles. Sardarji believed him and visited this Sadhu unarmed. The Sadhu gave him some herbs to prepare and brought the police in the meanwhile. Sardar Saheb was arrested. That Sadhu was an inspector of the CID department. The Babbar Akalis stepped up their activities. Many pro-government men were killed. The doab land lying in between Beas and Sutlej, that is, the districts of Jullundur and Hoshiarpur, had been there on the political map of the country, even before this. The majority of martyrs of 1915 belonged to these districts. Now again, there was the upheaval. The police department used all its power at its command, which proved quite useless. There is a small river near Jullundur; "Chaunta Sahib" Gurudwara is located there in a village on the banks of the river. There Shri

Karam Singhji, Shri Dhanna Singhji, Shri Uday Singhji and Shri Anoop Singhji were sitting with a few others, preparing tea. All of a sudden, Shri Dhanna Singhji said: "Baba Karam Singhji! We should at once leave this place. I sense something very inauspicious happening." The 75-year-old Sardar Karam Singh showed total indifference, but Shri Dhanna Singhji left the place, along with his 18-year-old follower Dilip Singh. Quite suddenly Baba Karam Singh stared at Anoop Singh and said: "Anoop Singh, you are not a good person", but after this, he himself became unmindful of his own premonition. They were still talking when police made a declaration: Send out the rebels, otherwise the village will be burnt down. But the villagers did not yield.

Seeing all this, they themselves came out. Anoop Singh ran with all the bombs and surrendered. The remaining four people were standing, surrounded from all sides. The British police captain said: "Karam Singh! drop the weapons and you will be pardoned." The hero responded challengingly: "We will die a martyr's death while fighting, as a real revolutionary, for the sake of our motherland, but we shall not surrender our weapons." He inspiringly called his comrades. They also roared like lions. A fight ensued. Bullets flew in all directions. After their ammunition exhausted, these brave people jumped into the river and bravely died after hours of ceaseless fighting.

Sardar Karam Singh was 75 years old. He had been in Canada. His character was pure and behaviour ideal. The government concluded that the Babbar Akalis were finished, but actually they grew in strength. The 18-year-old Dilip Singh was a very handsome and strong, well-built, though illiterate, young man. He had joined some dacoit gang. His association with Shri Dhanna Singhji turned him from a dacoit into a real revolutionary. Many notorious dacoits like Banta Singh and Variyam Singh, too, gave up dacoity and joined them.

There were not afraid of death. They were eager to wash their old sins. They were increasing in number day-by-day. One day when Dhanna Singh was sitting in a village named. Mauhana, the police were called. Dhanna Singh was down with drinks and caught without resistance. His revolver was snatched, he was handcuffed and brought out. Twelve policemen and two British officers had surrounded him. Exactly at that moment there was a thunderous noise of explosion. It was the bomb exploded by Dhanna Singhji. He died on the spot along with one British officer and ten policemen. All the rest were badly wounded.

In the same fashion, Banta Singh, Jwala Singh and some others were surrounded in a village named Munder. They all were gathered on the roof of a house. Shots were fired, a crossfire ensued for some time, but then the police sprinkled kerosene oil by a pump and put the house on fire. Banta Singh was killed there, but Variyam Singh escaped even from there.

It will not be improper here to describe a few more similar incidents. Banta Singh was a very courageous man. Once he snatched a horse and a rifle from the guard of the armoury in the Jullundur Cantonment. Those days several police squads were desperately looking for him; one such squad confronted him somewhere in the forest. Sardar Saheb challenged them immediately: "If you have courage, come and confront me." On that side, there were slaves of money; on this side, the willing sacrifice of life. There was no comparison of motives. The police squad beat a retreat.

This was the condition of the special police squads deputed to arrest them. Anyway, arrests had become a routine. Police checkposts were erected in almost every village. Gradually, the Babbar Akalis were weakened. Till now it had seemed as if they were the virtual rulers. Wherever they happened to be visiting, they were warmly hosted, by some with fear and terror. The supporters of the regime were defeatist. They lacked the courage to move out of their residences between the sunset and the sunrise. They were the 'heroes' of the time. They were brave and their worship was believed to be a kind of hero worship, but gradually they lost their strength. Hundreds among them were imprisoned, and cases were instituted against them.

Variyam Singh was the lone survivor. He was moving towards Layallpur, as the pressure of police had increased in Jullundur and Hoshiarpur. One day he was hopelessly surrounded there, but he came out fighting valiantly. He was very much exhausted. He was alone. It was a strange situation. One day he visited his maternal uncle in the village named Dhesian. Arms were kept outside. After taking his meals, he was moving towards his weaponry when the police arrived. He was surrounded. The British officer caught him from the backside. He wounded him badly with his kripan (sword), and he fell down. All the efforts to handcuff him failed. After two years of suppression, the Akali Jatha came to an end. Then the cases started, one of which has been discussed above. Quite recently too, they had wished to be hanged soon. Their wish has been fulfilled; they are now quiet.

3

Religious Riots and Their Solution
(June, 1927)

In the aftermath of the 1919 Jallianwala Bagh tragedy, Hindu and Muslims were caught in communal tension leading to riots in Kohat in 1924. This essay critiques the role of religious and political leaders, as well as the media, in perpetuating these conflicts. The essay *'Dharmvar Fasad Te Unha de Ilaj'* (Religious Riots and their Solution) was initially published in Punjabi in the June 1927 issue of *Kirti*.

Translation by Dr Hina Nandrajog.

The condition of India is indeed pitiable today. The devotees of one religion are sworn enemies of the devotees of another religion. Merely to belong to one religion is now considered enough reason to be the enemy of another religion. If we find this difficult to believe, let us look at the fresh outbreaks of violence in Lahore. How the Muslims killed innocent Sikhs and Hindus, and how even the Sikhs did their worst when the opportunity came. This butchering was not done because a particular man committed a crime, but because a particular man is a Hindu or a Sikh or a Muslim. Just the fact of a person being a Sikh or a Hindu is enough for him to be killed by a Muslim, and in the same way, merely being a Muslim is sufficient reason to take his life. If this is the situation, then may God help Hindustan!

Under these conditions, the future of Hindustan seems very bleak. These 'religions' have ruined the country. And one has no idea how long these religious riots will plague Hindustan. These riots have shamed Hindustan in the eyes of the world. And we have seen how everyone is carried upon the tide of blind faith. It is a rare Hindu, Muslim or

Sikh who can keep a cool head; the rest of them take sticks and staffs, swords and knives and kill each other. Those who escape death either go to the gallows or are thrown into jail. After so much bloodshed, these 'religious' folk are subjected to the baton of the English government, and only then do they come to their senses.

As far as we've seen, communal leaders and newspapers are behind these riots. These days the Indian leaders exhibit such shameful conduct that it is better not to say anything. The same leaders who have taken upon themselves the challenge of winning independence for their country and who don't tire of shouting slogans of 'Common Nationality' and 'Self Rule… Self-Rule…' are hiding themselves and are flowing with this tide of religious blindness. The number of people hiding themselves is much less. But leaders who join communal agitations can be found in hundreds when one scratches the surface. There are very few leaders who wish for the welfare of people from the bottom of their hearts. Communalism has come like such a great deluge that they are not able to stem it. It appears as if the leadership of Bharat has gone bankrupt.

The other people who have played a special role in igniting communal riots are the newspaper people.

The profession of journalism that, at one point of time, was accorded a very high status has become very filthy now. These people print prominent, provocative headlines and rouse the passions of people against one another, which leads to rioting. Not just in one or two places, but in many places riots have taken place because the local papers have written very outrageous essays. Few writers have been able to maintain their sanity and keep calm on such days.

The real duty of the newspapers was to impart education, eradicate narrowmindedness in people, put an end to communal feelings, encourage mutual understanding and create a common Indian nationalism. But they have turned their main business to spread ignorance, preach narrowness, create prejudice, lead to rioting and destroy Indian common nationalism. This is the reason that tears of blood flow from our eyes at Bharat's present state and the question that rises in our heart is, 'What will become of Hindustan?'.

The people who are familiar with the enthusiasm and awakening of the times during the non-cooperation movement feel like crying at this present state. What days those were when they could glimpse independence in front of them—and today! The idea of Home Rule seems like a mere dream now. That is the advantage that the tyrants have got from communal riots. The bureaucracy that had begun to fear for its very existence has now dug in its roots so deeply that it is not an easy task to shake it.

If we look for the roots of these communal riots, the reason seems to be economic. Leaders and journalists went through untold sacrifices during the days of the non-cooperation movement. They suffered financially as well. When the movement ebbed, it led to a lack of confidence in the leaders, which led to the collapse of the business of a lot of these religious leaders. The question of filling one's belly is at the bottom of whatever work is done in this world. This is one of the three principal maxims of Karl Marx. It is due to this maxim that Hindu-Muslim community practices like the Tablig, Tanzeem, Shuddhi, etc., were initiated, and it is because of this that we are in such a terrible state; in this mess.

If there is to be any lasting solution to all these communal riots, it lies only in the improvement of the economic condition of Hindustan; because the economic condition of the common people is so degraded in Hindustan, that anyone can pay four annas to get another person insulted. Tormented by hunger and sorrow, a person can abandon all principles. It becomes a matter of survival.

But economic reforms are too difficult in the present circumstances because the government is a foreign one and it does not allow any improvement in the condition of the people. That is why people must concentrate all their energy on attacking it and not rest till it is completely transformed.

Class-consciousness is crucial to stop people from fighting each other. The poor workers and peasants should be made to clearly understand that their real enemies are the capitalists, so they must be careful not to fall into their trap. All the poor people of the world—whatever their caste, race, religion, or nation—have the same rights. It is in your interest that all discrimination on account of religion, colour, race, and nationality is eliminated and the power of the government be taken in your hands. These efforts will not harm you in any way, but will one day cut off your shackles and you will get economic freedom.

The people who are familiar with the history of Russia know that similar conditions prevailed there during the rule of the Tsar. There were several groups who kept dragging each other down. But from the day the Workers' Revolution took place, the very map of the place changed. Now there are never any riots there. Now everyone is considered to be a 'human being' there, not 'a member of a religious group'. The economic condition of the people was very pathetic during the times of the Tsar and this led to rioting. But now when the economic condition of the Russians has improved and they have developed class-consciousness, there is no news about any riots from there.

Though one hears very heart-rending accounts of such riots, yet one heard something positive about the Calcutta riots. The workers of the trade unions did not participate in the riots nor did they come to blows with each other; on the other hand, all the Hindus and Muslims behaved normally towards each other in the mills and even tried to stop the riots. This is because there was class consciousness in them and they fully recognized what would benefit their class. This is the beautiful path of class-consciousness that can stop communal rioting.

We have received this bit of happy news that the youth of Bharat are now tired of religions that teach mutual hatred and war, and are washing their hands off such religions; and there is so much progressiveness in them now that they look upon the people of Bharat, not from the point of view of religion—as Hindu, Muslim, or Sikh—but human beings first, and then as citizens of one country. The birth of such feelings in the youth of Bharat gives us hope for a golden future and the people of Bharat should not worry about these riots; they should rather hold themselves in a state of readiness and always attempt to ensure that such an environment is not created; that there are no riots ever.

In 1914-15, the martyrs separated religion from politics. They believed that religion was an individual's personal matter and no one else should interfere in it. Nor should one let religion push itself into politics because it does not unite everyone or make them work together. That is the reason movements like the Ghadar Party were strong and shared a single goal in which the Sikhs were at the forefront for going to the gallows, and even the Hindus and the Muslims didn't lag behind.

At present, some Indian leaders also want to separate religion from politics. This is also a beautiful remedy to eliminate quarrels and we support it.

If religion is separated from politics, then we can all come together in politics, even if we belong to different religions.

We think that the real sympathizers of Hindustan will ponder over our prescribed remedy and that we will save India from self-destruction.

We hope that class-consciousness shall also emerge among the workers and peasants of organizations that the Congress party has adopted, because this will hasten the elimination of communal riots.

4

Religion and Our Freedom Struggle
(May, 1928)

In this essay, Bhagat Singh talks about a political conference that was held in Amritsar in 1928 by the members of the Naujawan Bharat Sabha and how the issue of religion was a heated topic of discussion. The essay questions the role of religion in politics, argues against its divisive influence and advocates for freedom from religious dogma to achieve true unity and independence in India. The essay makes some concrete suggestions for unity among the people of India. The essay 'Mazhab te Sadi Azadi di Jang' (Religion and Our Freedom Struggle) was originally written in Punjabi and published in the May 1928 issue of *Kirti*.

Translation by Dr Hina Nandrajog.

A political conference was held in Amritsar from April 11 to 13, 1928, along with the conference for the youth. A great deal of debate and discussion centred around two or three points. One of the issues was religion. Though no one would have raised the question of religion yet a resolution was proposed against communal organizations, and those who were supporting these communal organizations under the pretext of religion wanted to protect themselves. This question could have remained buried a little longer; but once it was brought to the public arena, discussion regarding it could take place and the concomitant question of solving the issue of religion also arose. Even in the subject committee of the regional conference when Maulana Zafar Ali Sahib uttered *'Khuda, Khuda!'* a few times, the President, Pandit Jawaharlal, asked him to refrain from doing so on that platform. 'If you are a missionary of religion, then I am a preacher of irreligion'. Later, even in Lahore a meeting of Naujawan Bharat Sabha was held. Several speeches were made and advice dispensed by some gentlemen who used religion for their benefit and also by those who were afraid to discuss this divisive issue, lest it led to tension.

The most important thing that was reiterated repeatedly and upon which Shriman Bhai Amar Singhji Jhabaal laid special emphasis was that the question of religion should not be touched at all. This was very good advice. If anyone's religion is not creating an obstacle in another person's happiness and peace, then why should anyone have a reason to raise a voice against it? But the question that arises is this: what has experience taught us till now? Even in the last agitation, the same question of religion had arisen and every one had been given complete freedom. So much so that mantras and aayats began to be read from the Congress days as well. Those days anyone lagging behind in religion was not considered to be good. As a result, narrow-mindedness was on the rise.

The ill effects of this are not hidden from anyone. Now the nationalist people and lovers of freedom have grasped the truth behind religion and think of it as an obstacle in their path.

The moot point is that even if one keeps one's religion a private matter, does it not heighten a feeling of alienation in people's hearts? Does it not affect the aim of attaining complete freedom for the country? At this time, the worshippers of complete freedom call religion a kind of mental slavery. They also feel that telling a child that God is omnipotent and man nothing but a mere statue of clay, is to make the child weak forever. It is to destroy the strength of his heart and his sense of self-confidence. But even if we don't discuss this and go straight to the direct questions before us, we see that religion is an obstacle in our path. For example, we want everyone to be equal. There should be no division of class among the capitalists, nor of touchable and 'untouchable'. But Sanatan Dharma is in favour of this discrimination. Even in the twentieth century, if a low-caste boy garlands people like the Pandit or the Maulvi, they have a bath with their clothes on and refuse to grant the *janeyu*, the sacred thread, to the 'untouchables'. Either we pledge to say nothing against this religion and sit silently at home or we must oppose it. People also say that we must reform these ills. Very good! Swami Dayanand abolished untouchability but he could not go beyond the four varnas. Discrimination still remained. If the Sikhs go to the Gurudwara and sing *'Raj Karega Khalsa (May the Khalsa rule!)'* and then come out and talk of a Republic, what meaning does it have?

Religion says that the kafirs that don't follow Islam should be hacked down; what would be the result if an exhortation of unity is given here? We are aware that chanting some higher order aayats and mantras can be used to draw different interpretations but the question is why should we not rid ourselves of this entire problem? Religion stands before us like a mountain. Suppose a freedom struggle spread all over the country, armies with guns stand face-to-face, shots are about to be fired and if at that moment someone does what Mohammed Ghori did—as the story goes—and even today places cows, pigs, the Granth Sahib, Veda–Quran, etc., before us, then what will we do? If we are staunchly religious, we will roll up our beddings and go back home. While there is religion, Hindus and Sikhs will not shoot at cows or Muslims at a pig. Staunch believers would keep rolling in front of their idols like the thousands of priests at the Somnath Temple, while the others, atheists or the irreligious, will get the task done. So, what conclusion do we reach? One is forced to think against religion. But let us even consider the argument offered by those in favour of religion, who say that the world would become a land of darkness and sin will increase if religion is absent. All right, let us look at this.

The Russian Mahatma, Tolstoy, writing about religion in his *Essays and Letters* has divided it into three parts:

1. Essentials of Religion, that is, the main tenets of religion—to speak the truth, not steal, help the poor, stay in harmony with others, etc.

2. Philosophy of Religion, that is, the philosophy of birth and death, reincarnation, the creation of the world, etc. In this, a person tries to think and understand things according to his own will.

3. Rituals of Religion, for example the rites and conventions, etc.

This means that in the first part, all religions are alike. All believe in speaking the truth, not lying, living in harmony with others. Some people have called these things Individual Religion. There is no question of dissent here. In fact, every human being should follow such noble principles. The second is the question of philosophy. One has to accept that 'Philosophy is the outcome of human weakness'. Where people can see, there is no trouble. When things are not clearly visible, then one's brain works overtime and some specific results are dug out. Philosophy is undoubtedly a very important thing because we cannot progress without it, yet peace is equally important. Our elders have said that there is reincarnation, but the Christians and Muslims don't believe in it. Very well, to each his own! Come, let us sit down and discuss this calmly. Learn each other's views. But when there is a debate on the question of the transmigration of the soul, then the Arya Samajis and the Muslims come to blows. The thing is that both parties lock up their intelligence and abandon their power to think and debate. They believe that God has written this in the Veda in this manner—and that is the ultimate truth. The others believe that in the Quran Sharif, God has written this—and that this is the only truth. These people have abandoned all powers of reasoning. If philosophy had no greater power than the personal opinion of an individual and no separate groups are formed due to a belief in a particular philosophy, what is there to complain about?

Now, we come to the third thing—the rituals. On the day of Saraswati Pooja, it is necessary to take Goddess Saraswati's idol in a procession and it is also necessary that a band be brought to play music before the idol. But en route there is a mosque on Harrison Road. Islam says that there should be no music in front of a mosque. Now, what should be done? Civil rights of a citizen decree that one can go through the market playing music, but religion says no. In one religion, cow sacrifice is prescribed and in the other, cow worship. What to do under the circumstances? If religion undergoes a change as soon as a bough of a peepal tree is cut, what should be done? And these minor differences in philosophy and rituals and customs later grow into a National Religion and become the reason for the making of separate organizations. The result is before us to see.

So, if religion is to mix superstition with the above-written third and second thing, then there is no need for religion. Not tomorrow, rather it should be blown up today itself! If free thought can be mixed with the first and second, then may such a religion flourish! But it is necessary to do away with factionalism and discrimination in the serving and sharing of food; words like 'untouchables' will have to be uprooted entirely.

Till the time we do not let go of our narrow-mindedness and become one, true unity cannot be achieved. So, only by following the above-mentioned things can we move towards freedom. Our freedom does not mean merely to escape the hold of the British; it means complete independence—when people will intermingle with each other freely and be rid of mental slavery as well.

5

The Issue of Untouchability
(June, 1928)

The essay, originally written in Punjabi as *'Achhoot da Sawaal'* and published in *Kirti* in June 1928 under the name *'Vidrohi'*, critiques the caste system and untouchability in India. It condemns the discriminatory treatment of 'untouchables' and advocates their empowerment through organization and activism, and calls for a revolution against the oppressive social and economic structures, emphasizing unity and self-reliance.

Translation by Dr Hina Nandrajog.

In no other country except ours does such a bad state of affairs prevail. Strange and peculiar questions keep arising here. One crucial question is that of the 'untouchables'. The problem is that in a population of thirty crores, there are six crore people who are called 'untouchables', i.e., their mere touch will pollute the dharma of the rest. Their entry into temples would displease the Gods. Drawing water from wells would make the water of these wells impure. These questions are being raised in the twentieth century and one is ashamed even to listen to these questions.

Our country is very spiritual, yet we hesitate to give the status of a human being to a person, while the West, referred to as being completely materialistic, has been raising the banner of oneness for centuries. The West declared equality as a principle in the American and French Revolutions. Today, Russia has resolved to eradicate every kind of discrimination, fulfilling the ideals pledged on the first of May. We are forever bothered about the being of soul and God, and involved in a strident debate about whether we should grant the *janeyu*, the sacred thread, to the 'untouchable' or do they have the right to study the Vedas and the scriptures or not? We complain that we are not treated well in other countries. The British government does not consider us at par with the English, but do we have the right to make this complaint?

A Muslim gentleman from Sindh, Shri Noor Mohammed, a member of the Bombay Council has spoken at length about this in 1926: "If the Hindu Society refuses to allow other human beings, fellow creatures so that to attend public schools, and if... the president of local board representing so many lakhs of people in this house refuses to allow his fellows and brothers the elementary human right of having water to drink, what right have they to ask for more rights from the bureaucracy? Before we accuse people coming from other lands, we should see how we ourselves behave toward our own people.... How can we ask for greater political rights when (we ourselves) deny elementary rights to human beings?"

What he says is absolutely right, but because it has been said by a Muslim, the Hindus will say, 'Look! He wants to convert the 'untouchables' to Islam and assimilate them in their fold.'

If you consider them worse than beasts, then certainly they will embrace other religions where they will be given better rights and where they will be treated like human beings. Then to lament, 'Just see, the Christians and the Muslims are harming the Hindu community!' would be futile.

How true is this statement but everyone is enraged at it. Exactly this anxiety gripped the Hindus as well. Even the Sanatan Dharma scholars have begun to ponder over this problem. At times, those who are known as great revolutionaries joined in. In the conference of the Hindu

Mahasabha in Patna, which was held under the aegis of Lala Lajpat Rai as President—an old supporter of the 'untouchables'—a sharp debate began. There were a lot of clashes. The problem was whether the 'untouchables' had the right or not to perform *yagyopavit*, the Hindu ceremony of wearing the sacred thread. And did they have the right to study the scriptures and the Vedas or not? Great, well-known social reformers were incensed but Lalaji made everyone concur; and redeemed Hindu dharma by accepting both these things. Otherwise, just think how shameful it would have been. A dog can sit in our lap. He can roam freely in our kitchen but we become polluted if a human being touches us! Now, a great social reformer like Pandit Malviyaji, a great champion of the 'untouchables', and what not, can be garlanded by a scavenger but considers himself to be impure unless he has a bath with his clothes on afterwards. What a great swindle! Make a temple to worship the God who loves everyone; but if an 'untouchable' enters it, it becomes defiled. God becomes angry. If this is the state of affairs at home, is it seemly to fight for equal rights abroad? Then our behaviour reveals only an extremity of ingratitude. We shun the very people who do the lowliest of work to provide us with facilities. We can worship beasts but cannot make a human being sit next to us.

Today, there is a great deal of hue and cry over this issue. Those ideas are being especially discussed these days. The communal feelings may or may not have done any good to enhance the freedom struggle in the country, but at least it has given one advantage. Everyone is anxious to increase the numbers of their community to ask for better rights. The Muslims made a little extra effort. They converted the 'untouchables' to Islam and gave them equal rights. This hurt the pride of the Hindus. Hostility grew, which even led to riots. Gradually, even the Sikhs thought that they should not be left behind. They also began to baptize them. Hindus and Sikhs fought over the taking off of the *janeyu* and the cutting of hair. Now, all three communities are drawing the 'untouchables' into their fold. So, there is a lot of hue and cry. On the other side, the Christians are quietly enhancing their status. Anyway, all this activity is erasing this slur on the country.

And when the 'untouchables' saw how everyone was fighting over them and thought of them as fodder, they reflected on why they should not unite by themselves. Whether the English had any hand in this idea or not is not clear, but it is certain that there was considerable use of government machinery in the propagation of this idea. Organizations like Adi Dharma Mandal are a result of this idea.

Now, another question that arises is what the correct solution to this problem should be. The answer to this is very simple. First of all, it should be decided that all human beings are equal and no one is different either at birth or through division of labour. That is, just because a man has been born in the house of a poor sweeper, he will end up spending the rest of his life cleaning the toilets of others and have no right in the world to progress—all this is rubbish. This is the cruel manner in which our Aryan ancestors treated them, stigmatizing them as low-caste and making them do lowly tasks. Along with this, there was an anxiety, lest they revolt. Then the philosophy of reincarnation was propagated to show that it was the fruit of their sins in past lives. So, what can be done? Spend your days quietly. By preaching patience to them in this manner, they managed to silence the unprivileged for a long time. But they committed a grave sin. They erased humanity from human beings. A lot of oppression and cruelty was inflicted. Now is the time to atone for our sins.

Another problem arose along with this. Abhorrence for essential tasks arose in the minds of the people. We spurned the weaver. Today, even weavers are considered 'untouchables'. In the region of the United Provinces, even pallbearers are considered 'untouchables'. This has led to a lot of mess being created. This is proving to be detrimental to the process of progress.

Keeping these communities in mind, we need to neither call them 'untouchables' nor think of them as being so. And the problem would be solved! The strategy that Naujawan Bharat Sabha and the youth conference has adopted is quite a good one. We should ask for forgiveness of those who have been called 'untouchables'. and consider them to be equal human beings like us, without being given *amrit*, without reciting the *kalma* or being purified, and count them among ourselves, to take water from their hands; that is the right course. And to fight amongst ourselves and not to give any rights to them is not the correct approach.

When the propagation of labour rights began in villages, the government officials tried to mislead the Jat peasants by saying that pampering the low castes would affect their work adversely. And that was enough! The Jat peasants were incensed. They must remember that their condition cannot improve till the time they want to keep these poor people under their thumb by terming them as low-born and mean. It is often said that they are not clean. The answer is clear— they are poor. Treat poverty. The poor in the high castes also don't stay clean. Even the pretext of doing dirty work cannot be taken because mothers clean the shit of children and don't become 'untouchable' or of low caste.

But this cannot be accomplished till the time the 'untouchables' organize themselves. We consider it to be a very positive movement that they are organizing themselves voluntarily or because they are equal in numbers to the Muslims and thus asking for equal rights. Either end this problem of communal discrimination or give them their separate rights. The duty of the Councils and the Assemblies is to ensure complete freedom to these people to use schools and colleges, wells and roads. Not just by lip service, but actually take them to the wells. Get their children admitted to schools. But in the Legislature where the Bill against child marriage and religion creates such public outrage, how can they muster the courage to assimilate the 'untouchables' within the community?

So, we say that they must have their representatives. They must demand more rights for themselves. We clearly say— Rise, brothers who are called 'untouchables' and are the real servants of the people! Rise, look at your history. You were the real strength of Guru Gobind Singh's army. It was due to you that Shivaji was able to do so much; due to you that his name lives on today. Your sacrifices are etched in golden letters. You are doing us a great favour by rendering your services daily, adding to the comfort of the lives of the public and making life possible, and we people do not understand that. According to the Land Alienation Act, you cannot even buy land by saving money. You are so oppressed that the American, Miss Mayo, exhorts you to rise and recognize your strength. To get organized. In reality, without making your own efforts, you will get nothing. 'Those who would be free must themselves strike the blow'. Those who want freedom must fight for independence. Gradually, human beings have developed a habit of wanting greater rights for themselves, but to keep those under them, oppressed. So, those who understand the language of punches don't understand words. That is, organize and stand on your own feet and challenge the entire world. Then you will see that no one will dare to deny you your rights. Don't become fodder for others. Don't look at others for help. But beware, don't be trapped by bureaucracy. They don't want to help you at all but want to make you their pawns. This capitalist bureaucracy is the real reason behind your slavery and poverty. So, make sure that you never join them. Be wary of their wiles. Everything will become all right then.

You are the real working class. Workers unite. You have nothing to lose except chains. Rise and rebel against the present system. Gradual, slow reforms will lead you nowhere. Create a revolution with a social agitation and tighten your belts for a political and economic revolution. You are the foundation of the country; the real strength. Arouse the sleeping lions! Rise and revolt!

6

Satyagraha and Strikes
(June, 1928)

The essay discusses the resurgence of Satyagraha and strikes in 1928 India, focussing on the Bardoli peasant Satyagraha against unjust tax hikes. It also highlights strikes in various industries demanding better wages and working conditions. The essay, published in June 1928, underscores the significance of the grassroots movements in the freedom struggle.

Translation by Dr Hina Nandrajog.

Satyagraha

Life again seems to have been infused into Hindustan in 1928. On the one hand, there are general strikes and on the other, preparations are underfoot for Satyagraha. These are very good signs. The biggest Satyagraha is being held by the peasants of Bardoli (in Gujarat). After every 30 years, taxes are revised and every time the tax on the land is raised. The same thing happened this year as well and the tax has been hiked. What are people to do? The poor peasant in any case is not able to fill his belly so how can he pay 22 percent tax more than before? Preparations were made for Satyagraha. Mahatma Gandhi corresponded with the Governor of Punjab to try and get the tax reduced, but Sir, this government is not about to bend only through letters. It had no effect. The people had to go on a Satyagraha. Even earlier, on a few occasions, the peasants had gone on a Satyagraha in Gujarat and defeated the government. Earlier, in 1917-18, the crop had rotted due to excessive rains and was not even worth one fourth of the price of the normal crop. The law stated that tax would not be collected if the crop was less than six annas worth in a rupee and it would be collected along with the next year's tax. That year when the people protested that they did not have even four annas worth of crop, the government did not heed their word. Then Mahatma Gandhiji took the matter into his hands and held a meeting. He explained to the people that if they refused to pay the tax their land would be confiscated, and asked them if they were prepared for that. The people kept quiet and the Satyagraha leaders from Bombay became upset and got up to leave. But then an old farmer got up and said that they would endure everything, and then the others also began to concur with him. Satyagraha began. The government began to confiscate the land and property, but after two months, the government was forced to blink first and accede to the conditions set by the landlords.

The second Satyagraha took place in 1923-24, when Mahatmaji was in jail. The first time 600 villages had taken part. This time the tax of 94 villages was raised and these villages went on Satyagraha. A punitive tax was imposed on them. There was a law that no property could be attached after sunset and the peasants would lock up their houses early in the morning and leave, so the police would not find a single person as a witness. Finally, the government got fed up and revoked the tax. This time the Satyagraha has begun in Bardoli. In 1921-22, intense preparations had been made in Bardoli to Satyagraha for freedom. All a game of chance! All preparations went to naught. Anyway, why brood over the past now? Now the government fixed the tax in that area. The poor farmers! Land tax was raised by 22 percent. A lot of protests took place, but was the government about to listen? Work began under the leadership of Shri Vallabh Bhai Patel and the farmers refused to pay the tax. Now all the Recovery Officers and government officials have gathered together in Bardoli area. They are doing whatever they can to misguide these people. Property is being attached; orders are being given to confiscate land. But there is no one to carry the stuff. These days there is a lot of activity there but one interesting thing is that everything is being done very peacefully. The officers, who had come to trouble the farmers, are being dealt with very cordially. Earlier they did not get food and water, now, the Headman said that they must be given food and water. One day four containers were impounded from the liquor shop, but there was no one to carry them. When the officer said, "I'm very thirsty; at least give me some water," then immediately a volunteer satyagrahi brought a bottle of soda for him. So the action is on at great speed, but very peacefully. There are high hopes that the government will bow down finally.

The other place where the Satyagraha is to take place is Kanpur. There were Hindu–Muslim riots in the last few days in Kanpur. Later, a disciplinary force was put on duty. A few days ago, Shri Ganesh Shankarji Vidyarthi, a member of the Kanpur Council and the editor of the newspaper *Pratap*, received a letter from a magistrate that he should prepare a list of all employees with details of their designations and salary, because punitive tax was to be collected. But Vidyarthiji wrote back to say that he was not prepared to pay any tax; nor would he render any assistance in this task because it was the police that was responsible for the riots. The people should not be punished for the police's crime. The people asked Vidyarthiji, 'What should we do?' and he answered, 'There will be trouble, a lot of damage will be done, but we should not pay this unreasonable tax.' Processions were held. 7,000 people signed a petition that they would not pay the tax and sent it to the government. Preparations are being made.

The third place is Meerut. There, too, the land tax was revised and raised. Satyagraha has been proclaimed there as well.

Even in Punjab, signs of something similar are visible. The crops in Sheikhupura and Lahore districts have been ruined due to hailstorms. There is hardly any harvest, so how can they pay the tax? But the wise and intelligent people of this region are speaking a different language—'Let not the "disreputable" people of the Congress give speeches to the farmers, lest the government gets annoyed.' Such things are happening, but it should be remembered that 'those who understand the language of punches, don't understand words'. The British understand only the language of money and to expect that they would voluntarily take back the tax! Till when will this illusion remain?

Strikes

On the one hand, Satyagraha is making waves, and on the other, strikes are playing a no less important role. It is a very happy thing that there is life again in the nation and the war of the peasants and the workers has begun for the first time. This will impact the forthcoming movement. These are really the people who deserve freedom. The peasant and the worker demand food and their demand will not be met till one has attained complete freedom. They cannot stop at the Round Table Conference or any other such thing. Anyway! These days, the Liluah Railway Workshop, the Tata Mills in Jamshedpur, the sweeper class in Jamshedpur and the textile mills in Bombay have gone on strike. In fact, the main demands of most people are the same. Low wages, gruelling work, and bad treatment. The poor eke out an existence as best as they can under the circumstances, but it finally becomes unendurable. Today, there are about a lakh and a half people on strike in Bombay. Only one mill is functioning. The fact is that new looms have been bought; in which one person has to work on two looms and, thus, has to put in double the effort. The demands include raising the wages of such workers specially, but also ask for an increase in the salaries of all the workers and a stipulation of not more than 8 hours of work. These days, strikes are popular. The Jamshedpur mill workers have similar demands. The strikes are on the rise there as well. The scavengers are on strike and the entire city is in a mess. We do not allow these brothers who serve us the maximum to come close to us, cast them off calling them 'scavenger-scavenger' and take advantage of their poverty, and make them work for very low wages, and even without wages! Great! Finally, these people are bound to rise against this. They can bring the people, especially in the cities, to their knees in just a couple of days. Their awakening is a happy development. Some people were fired from the Liluah Workshop and there was some issue regarding wages, so they went on strike. Later, it was declared that the posts of several thousands of workers would be abolished and they would not be taken back even after the end of the strike. This created a sensation. But the strike is going strong. Gentlemen like Spratt are working very hard. People should support them in every way and put an end to the efforts being made to break the strike. We want that all the peasants and workers should unite and fight for their rights.

7

Students and Politics
(July, 1928)

The essay—written originally in Punjabi in *Kirti* in July 1928—criticizes Punjab's government and educators for discouraging student political engagement, arguing that education should cultivate civic awareness. It laments the shallow understanding of politics among students and advocates for their active participation, citing historical examples and emphasizing the youth's role in national liberation struggles.

Translation by Dr Hina Nandrajog.

A lot of noise is being made saying that students should not take part in political activities. The Punjab government's stand is most peculiar. Students are being made to sign an agreement that as a condition for admission in the college, they would not engage in political activities. On top of this, it is our misfortune that Manohar Lal, elected by the people, is now the Education Minister, who sends a circular to schools and colleges, decreeing that anyone studying or teaching shall not participate in political activities. A few days ago in Lahore, where the Students Union was celebrating the Student Week, Sir Abdul Qadir and Professor Ishwar Chandra Nanda emphasized that students should not get involved in politics.

Punjab is known to be the most backward in the political field. What is the reason for this? Have the sacrifices made by Punjab been too few? The reason is clear that our educated people are complete fools. Today, after reading the proceedings of the Punjab Council meeting, one has no doubts about the fact that our education system is rotten and useless, and young students, uncaring about the world around them, do not participate in national events. Nor do the students have any knowledge about such things. After completing their college education, only a few of them study further, but they talk in such an immature manner that one has no option but to bemoan such childishness. An attempt is being made today itself to make idiots out of the youth who will hold the reins of the country in the future. We should be able to understand the consequence of this. We agree that the main purpose for a student is to gain an education; they should direct all their energies to it, but is it not a part of education to develop the capacity to reflect upon the conditions in the country and think of ways to improve it? If not, then we consider such education as useless which should be acquired only to get a clerical job. What is the use of such education? Some over-clever people say, 'Kaka, you may certainly study and think about politics, but don't take any practical part in it. You will prove to be more beneficial to your nation by getting greater competence.'

This sounds beautiful but we tell you, this is only superficial talk. The following anecdote makes it clear. One day a student was reading a book, *An Appeal to the Young* by Prince Kropotkin. A learned Professor asked, "Which book is this? And this seems to be some Bengali name." The boy answered, 'Prince Kropotkin is very well known. He was a scholar in Economics.' It was very essential for every Professor to be familiar with this name. The student even laughed at the Professor's lack of knowledge. And then he added, "He was a Russian." That was enough. "Russian!" Catastrophic! The Professor said, "You are a Bolshevik because you read political books. I will immediately report you to the Principal!"

Look at the Professor's ability. Now, what is there for those poor students to learn from such people? What can those youths learn in such a situation?

The other thing is—what is practical politics? To welcome and listen to the speeches of Mahatma Gandhi, Jawaharlal Nehru and Subhas Chandra Bose is practical politics, but what about welcoming the Commission or the Viceroy? Is that not the other side of politics? Anything concerned with governments and nations would be considered a part of the political field. Would this be politics or not? Will it be said that the government would be pleased with this but displeased with that? Then the question is of the pleasure or displeasure of the government. Should students be taught the lesson of sycophancy right from birth? What we think is that till the time Hindustan is ruled by foreign thugs, the loyal are not loyal but traitors, not human beings, but beasts, slaves to their bellies. So how can we say that the students should learn the lesson of loyalty?

Everyone agrees that at this time Hindustan needs people who will sacrifice everything they have—body, mind and soul—to the country and shower everything in life like madmen upon their country. But can we find such people among the older people? Will people entangled in family and worldly affairs be able to come out? Only those young people can get involved who are not caught in any webs and students and young people can think of this before getting entangled, only if they have acquired some practical knowledge. If they have done more than just cramming for the Maths and Geography exams.

Was it not politics, when all the students in England left colleges to fight against Germany? Where were our advisors then to instruct them—'Go, go and get an education.' Today, will the students of National College Ahmedabad who are helping the Bardoli satyagrahis remain immature? Let us see how many competent people Punjab University produces as compared to them? It is the youth in all countries, who win freedom for their country. Can the youth of Hindustan save their identity and that of their country by staying indifferent? The youth cannot forget the tyrannies inflicted upon the students in 1919. They also understand that there is a need for a great revolution. Let them study; certainly let them study. But let them also acquire knowledge about politics and jump into the fray and devote their lives to it, when the need arises. Offer their lives to this cause. There seems to be no other way.

8

New Leaders and Their Different Ideas
(July, 1928)

The essay compares the leaders Subhas Chandra Bose and Jawaharlal Nehru, emphasizing their differing approaches to nationalism and revolution. It further explores Sadhu Vaswani's influence on the youth, Bose's emotionalism and Nehru's revolutionary stance, urging critical reflection for Punjab's youth. The essay was originally published in Punjabi in *Kirti* journal in July 1928.

Translation by Dr Hina Nandrajog.

A great deal of disappointment and despair spread among the people after the failure of the non-cooperation movement. Hindu–Muslim riots broke their remaining courage. But when awareness spreads in the countries once, the countries don't sleep. After a few days, they rise with great enthusiasm and launch an attack. Today, Hindustan is energized once again. Hindustan is gaining strength again. India is awakening again. Though a great movement is not visible, the foundations are definitely being strengthened. Several new leaders with new ideas are coming forward. This time it is the young leaders who are gaining visibility in the eyes of the patriotic, and there are active youth movements in the country. Eminent leaders are being pushed behind, despite being well-known.

At the moment, leaders who have come forward are Bengal's revered Shri Subhas Chandra Bose and respected Pandit Jawaharlal Nehru. These are the only two leaders who are visible today in Hindustan and are especially participating in the movements of the youth. Both of them are staunch supporters of freedom for Hindustan. Both are sensible men and true patriots. But there is a great deal of difference in their ideas. One of them is called a votary of Bharat's ancient culture, and the other is known as a true pupil of the West. One is called a soft-hearted sensitive man and the other a staunch revolutionary. In this essay, we shall present to the people their differing ideas, so that the people can appreciate the difference between them and can reflect upon them for themselves. But before elucidating the viewpoints of both of them, it is also important to present another person who is a lover of freedom as much as they are, and a special personality in youth movements—Sadhu Vaswani; even if he's not as well-known as the more popular names in the Congress; and even if he has no special place in the country's political field, he exerts an influence on the youth of the country who have to take the reins of the country in their hands tomorrow. 'Bharat Yuva Sangh', a movement begun by him, has a powerful impact on the youth. His ideas are completely novel. His ideas can be summed up in a few words—'Back to the Vedas'. Arya Samaj was the first to raise this slogan. The basis for this ideology is that God has poured in all the wisdom of the world into the Vedas. There can be no further evolution.

So, the world hasn't gone beyond, nor can it go beyond whatever progress our Hindustan had made in various fields. Anyway, people like Vaswani had faith in this. That's why at one place he says, "Our politics, until now, sometimes cites the examples of Mazzini and Voltaire as our ideals or has occasionally learnt lessons from Lenin and Tolstoy. Although they should know that they have even greater ideals before us—our ancient rishis." He believed that our country had reached the pinnacle of progress at least once, and today we have no need to go any further; in fact, we need to return to that. He is a poet. His poetic expression is evident everywhere in his thoughts. Moreover, he is a great devotee of religion. He wishes to propagate the religion of 'Shakti' or power. He says, "Our 'urgent' need is Shakti! At this stage we desperately need power." He does not use the word 'Shakti' only for power; he has faith in a kind of Devi; a faith in divine attainment. He says like a very passionate poet—"For in solitude we have communicated with her, our admired Bharat Mata, and my aching head has heard voices saying…. The day of freedom is not far off…. Sometimes indeed a strange feeling visits me and I say to myself, 'Holy, holy is Hindustan.' For still is she under the protection of her mighty rishis and their beauty is around us, but we behold it not." This is the lament of a poet; he bursts out like a madman or a devotee—"Our Mother is great. She is very powerful. Who has been born who can defeat her?" In this vein, he carries on flowing on a tide of emotion—"Our national movement must become a purifying mass movement if it is to fulfil its destiny without falling into class war—one of the dangers of Bolshevism." Just by mouthing words that one should go to the poor, or towards the villages, give them free medical aid, etc., they think that their job is done. He is a romantic poet. No specific meaning can be attributed to his poetry, but it can enthuse the heart. Apart from the cacophony of our ancient civilization he has no other programme. He offers nothing for the minds of our youth. He only wants to fill the hearts with emotion. He has a great influence over the youth; and this is on the rise. These are his summarized and conservative thoughts that we have described above.

Despite his ideas not having a direct effect in the political field, they wield considerable influence. Especially because these thoughts are being propagated among the youth; the young people who are to move ahead to the future. Now, we come to the thoughts of Shri Subhas Chandra Bose and Shri Jawaharlal Nehru. In the past few months, he has been made president of several conferences, and he presented his views before the people. The government considers Subhas Babu to be a member of a revolutionary group, and that is why he was kept in confinement under the Bengal Ordinance. He was released and became the leader of a radical faction. He considers complete freedom to be the ideal for India and he promoted this proposal in his Presidential Address at the Maharashtra Conference.

Pandit Jawaharlal Nehru is the son of Pandit Motilal Nehru, the leader of the Swaraj Party. He has cleared his Barrister's degree. He is very learned. He has toured Russia. He is also a member of the radical group, and it is with his support and that of his friends, that a resolution for 'Complete Independence' was passed in the Madras Conference. Even in the Amritsar Conference, he emphasized the same thing. But, even then, there is ample difference in the views of both these gentlemen.

The difference in their views became plain to us from their speeches during the Amritsar and Maharashtra Conference. But a lecture in Bombay later made it absolutely clear. Pandit Jawaharlal Nehru was the president of this conference and Subhas Chandra Bose delivered a speech. He is a very emotional Bengali. He began the speech by saying that Hindustan has a special message for the world. It will give the world spiritual education. Anyway, he began in a very enthused manner, 'Look at the Taj Mahal in the moonlight and imagine the greatness of the heart whose vision resulted in this.' Think, a Bengali novelist has written that they are our teardrops frozen into stone. He also exhorts one to return to the Vedas. In his speech in Poona, he spoke about 'Nationalism' and said that internationalists think of nationalists as narrow-minded, but this is an error. The idea of Hindustani Nationalism is different. It is neither narrow-minded, nor motivated by selfish interests, nor is it tyrannical because its base is *'Satyam Shivam Sundram'*, that is, 'Truth, Goodness, and Beauty'.

This is the same romanticism. Sheer emotionalism. And along with it, he too has a great deal of faith in our ancient civilization. In every little thing he glimpses the greatness of the ancient age. In his view, Republicanism is not a new concept. He says that Republics and Democracy are old concepts in Hindustan. He goes to the extent of saying that even Communism is not a new thing in Hindustan. Anyway, the thing that he emphasized the most in his speech that day was that Hindustan has a special message for the world.

Pandit Jawaharlal's ideas are completely different. He says, "Whichever country one visits, believes that she has a special message for the world. England claims to be the custodian to teach civilization to the world. I don't see anything special about my country. Subhas Babu has a lot of faith in such talk." Jawaharlal says, "Every youth must rebel. Not only in the political sphere, but in the social, economic and religious spheres also. I have not much use for any man who comes and tells me that such and such thing is said the Koran. Everything unreasonable must be discarded even if they find authority for it in the Vedas and Koran."

These are the views of a revolutionary and Subhas's views are that of a rebel. In the views of one of them, our ancient heritage is very good and, in the views of the other, one should revolt against it. One is called emotional, and the other, a revolutionary. At one point, Panditji says, "To those who still fondly cherish old ideas and are striving to bring back the conditions which prevailed in Arabia 1,300 years ago or in the Vedic age in India, I say that it is inconceivable that you can bring back the hoary past. The world of reality will not retrace its steps; the world of imagination may remain stationary." And that is why he feels the need for a revolution. Subhas Babu is in favour of complete independence because he says that the English inhabit the West and we, the East. Panditji says that we have to establish our rule and change the social system. For that, we must strive to win complete and total freedom.

Subhas Babu has sympathy for the workers and wishes to improve their condition. Panditji wants to bring about a change in the entire system. Subhas is sensitive—for the heart. He's giving a lot to the youth, but only for the heart. The other is a revolutionary, who is giving plenty for the head along with the heart. "They should aim at Swaraj for the masses based on socialism. That was a revolutionary change which they could not bring about without revolutionary methods.... Mere reform or gradual repairing of the existing machinery could not achieve the real proper Swaraj for the general masses."

This is an accurate picture of their views. Subhas Babu considered it necessary to pay attention to international politics only till world politics was concerned with the question of the security and development of Hindustan. But Panditji has traversed beyond the narrow circle of nationalism and entered a wider field.

Now, the issue is that we have both points of view before us. Which side should we bend towards? A Punjabi newspaper has eulogized about Subhas and, about Panditji it says that such revolutionaries beat their heads against stone walls and die. One should keep in mind that Punjab has always been a very emotional region. People become enthused very quickly and fall flat like froth equally swiftly.

Perhaps Subhas is not offering any mental stimulus, apart from some food for the heart. Now, the need is that the youth of Punjab should ponder and reflect upon these revolutionary ideas and reinforce them in their minds. At this point in time, Punjab is in dire need of mental stimulus and this is available only with Pandit Jawaharlal. This does not mean that we should follow him blindly. But as far as ideas are concerned, at this time the Punjabi youths should follow him so that they can learn the true meaning of revolution, the need for revolution in Hindustan, the place of revolution in the world, etc.

After proper reflection, the young people should evolve their own ideas so that even in times of disappointment, despair, and defeat, they should not get shaken and can stand alone if need be, to face the world. Only such people can make the revolution succeed.

9

What Is Anarchism – I, II, and III
(July, 1928)

These three essays were originally written in Punjabi by Bhagat Singh when he was working with the Punjabi journal, *Kirti*. They explore the concept of anarchism as a solution to global unrest, advocating for permanent peace through the elimination of government, religion, and private property. It discusses historical figures like Bakunin and Kropotkin who championed anarchist ideology through revolutionary actions.

Translation by Dr Hina Nandrajog.

Today, there is a lot of unrest in the world. Well-known scholars are engaged in establishing peace in the world; however, the peace that is sought to be established is not a temporary one but something that can be everlasting. Several great souls have sacrificed their lives to achieve it, and people continue to do so. But, today, we are slaves. Our eyesight is weak; our brains are dull. Our heart is weak and weeping over its weakness. How can we worry about world peace when we are not able to do anything for our own country? We can only call it our misfortune. We are being ruined by our own conservative ideas. We are trapped in the illusion of finding God and heaven, and seek redemption for our souls. We don't take more than an instant to refer to Europe as materialistic. We pay no attention to their great ideas. Because we are more inclined towards spiritual thought! Because we believe in renunciation! We should not even speak of this material world! We have come to such a pass that one wants to weep at the condition of the world, but the situation is improving in the twentieth century. European thought is beginning to make an impact on the youth's thinking. And the youth that wants to progress in the world should study the great and noble ideas of the modern age.

A person's knowledge is incomplete without understanding fully what voices are being raised in society today against oppression, or what ideas are being born for the establishment of permanent peace in the world. Today, we are listening to summarized versions of many ideas of communism and socialism, etc. Anarchism is thought to be the highest ideal among all these. This essay is being written regarding anarchism.

The people fear the word 'anarchist'. When a person rises to fight for his freedom, armed with a pistol or a bomb, then all the 'bureaucrats' and their underlings scream 'Anarchist-Anarchist!' and try to frighten the world. An anarchist is considered to be a very terrible person, who has no mercy in his heart, who sucks blood, who is delirious with joy at destruction and ruin. The word 'anarchist' has been given such a bad name that even the revolutionaries of India are referred to as anarchists to make people hate them. Dr Bhupindra Nath Dutt has mentioned this in the first part of his Bengali book *Unpublished Political History* saying that even if the government called them 'anarchist' to defame them, in truth they were a group of people who sought to usher in a new order. And anarchism is a very noble ideal. How was it possible for our common people to think of such a noble ideal, because they could not think of being revolutionaries beyond rebelling; of ushering in a new age. These people were merely rebels. Anyway!

As we mentioned earlier, the word 'anarchist' was given a bad name. This word was slandered in the same way that selfish capitalists slandered words like 'Bolshevik', 'Socialist', etc. Yet, anarchists are the most sensitive and ardent well-wishers of the entire world. Even if we disagree with their views, their sobriety, their love for the people, spirit of sacrifice and their genuineness cannot be doubted. The word 'anarchist' for which Hindi word *'araajak'* is used, is derived from a Greek word which literally means (an = not, arche = rule), that is, no government of any kind. Human beings always had a desire to be as free as possible, and from time to time, the idea of complete freedom, which is the principle of anarchism, has been mooted. For example, a long time ago, a Greek philosopher said, "We wish neither to belong to the governing class nor to the governed."

I consider that the feeling of world-fraternity in India and the Sanskrit phrase *'Vasudev Kutumbakam'* conveys the same sense. Even if we are unable to reach any conclusive proposition based on our ancient beliefs, we still have to believe that these thoughts were placed before, and openly propagated in, the world at the beginning of the nineteenth century (i.e., the last century) by a French philosopher, Proudhon. That is why he is called the father of anarchism. He began to propagate anarchism and later, one Russian brave man Bakunin did a lot of work to propagate and make it successful. Later, several anarchists like Johann Most and Prince Kropotkin were born. These days, Mrs Emma Goldman and Alexander Berkman propagate this in America. About anarchism, Mrs Goldman writes: "Anarchism—The philosophy of a new social order based on liberty unrestricted by man-made law. The theory that all forms of Government rest on violence, and are therefore wrong and harmful, as well as unnecessary."

This tells us that anarchists do not wish for any kind of government and this is true. But such a thought scares us.

Several bogies are raised in our minds. We should remain fearful of the ghosts of the preceding English rule even after setting up our own government and keep on trembling in fear—this is the policy of our rulers. Under such circumstances, how can we think even for one moment that such a day will dawn when we will be able to live happily and freely without a government? But this is, in fact, our own weakness. The ideal or the feeling is not to be blamed.

The ideal freedom that is imagined in anarchism is a complete liberation, according to which neither God nor religion should oppress our minds, nor should the temptation of money or the material world overtake us, or else the body could be shackled or controlled by some kind of governmental structure.

This means that broadly, they wished to completely eradicate three things from this world:

1. The Church, God (and religion)

2. The State (Government)

3. Private Property

This subject is very interesting and vast and much can be written about it, but we cannot stretch this essay too much due to paucity of space. So, we shall discuss the issues only broadly.

God and religion

Let us first consider God and religion. Now, even in Hindustan, voices are being raised against both these demons, but in Europe a revolution had risen in the last century itself. They begin with a reference to the age when people were ignorant; in those times, they were afraid of everything, especially supernatural powers. They completely lacked self-confidence and called themselves 'clay statues'. They say that religion, the supernatural and God are the result of the same ignorance, and that is why the illusion of their entity must be eliminated. Also, that from their very childhood, children are taught that God is everything—man is nothing.

Man is merely a statue of clay. Such thoughts crowding a person's mind erode his self-confidence. He begins to feel that he is very feeble. In this way, he is always fearful. Till the time this fear remains, complete happiness and peace cannot be attained.

In Hindustan, it was Gautam Buddha who first denied the existence of God. He had no belief in God. Even now there are a few ascetics who do not believe in the existence of God. Sohom Swami of Bengal is one such example. Recently, a book by Sohom Swami called *Common Sense* has been published in English. He has written robustly against the existence of God, trying to prove his proposition, but he does not become an anarchist. He does not wander about aimlessly using 'renunciation' and 'yoga' as pretexts. In this manner, the existence of God is being brought to an end in this scientific age, which will eradicate the very name of religion. In fact, the leader of the anarchists, Bakunin has thoroughly insulted God in his book *God and the State*. He placed the Biblical story and said that God made the world and man in his own image. Thank you very much! But he also warned against tasting the fruit of the forbidden tree of knowledge. Actually, God did create Adam and Eve for his own amusement, but he wanted them to remain his slaves forever and to never raise their head before him. So he gave them the gifts of the entire world but no intelligence. This state of affairs encouraged Satan to move forward—'but here steps in Satan, the eternal rebel, the first free thinker and the emancipator of the world'. He stepped forward, taught man to rebel and offered the fruit of the forbidden tree of knowledge. And that was enough for the omnipotent, omniscient God to lose his temper with a low-class, mean-minded mentality and he began to curse the world he himself had created. Wonderful!

The question that arises is why God made a world full of such sorrow. To enjoy the spectacle? In that case, he is more cruel than the Roman tyrant Nero. Is that his miracle? What is the need for such a miraculous God? The debate is growing. So, we'll conclude it right here by stating that religion has always been used by the selfish, the capitalists for their personal good. History bears witness to that. "Have patience!" "Look at your own deeds!" The havoc that such a philosophy has brought to mankind is evident for all to see.

People ask what would happen if we deny the existence of God? Sin would grow in the world. Chaos would reign. But the anarchists say that man would then grow to such a stature that without the greed of heaven and the fear of hell, he would shun bad deeds and begin to do good things. In actual fact, the reality is that in Hindustan, in *The Bhagavad Gita*, a world famous book, Shri Krishna, even while inspiring Arjuna to work selflessly without expectation of fruit lures him with visions of heaven after death and the crown of a king after victory in the battle. But, today, when we look at the sacrifices made by the anarchists, one wishes to kiss their feet. Sacco and Vanzetti's stories have been read by our readers. There is neither any desire to flatter God nor any avariciousness to enjoy the pleasures of heaven, nor any expectation of the bliss of reincarnation. To sacrifice one's life for the people and for truth with a smile on one's face is no small thing. The anarchists say that once people become completely liberated, their character will become very noble. Anyway, there can be long debates on each and every question, but we do not have enough space.

What Is Anarchism – II; 1928

The next thing they wish is to do away with is the government. If we look for the roots of political power, we arrive at two conclusions. Some people believe that the caveman's intelligence evolved gradually, and people began to live together in groups. Political power was born in this way. This is called the theory of evolution. The other theory is that people needed to get together and to organize in order to fight off wild animals and to fulfil other needs. Then these groups began to fight with each other and each one of them was afraid of the more powerful enemy. So people cooperated to establish a political order. This is called utilitarianism. We may pick both. The evolutionists can be asked why only now evolution has come to an end.

Panchayati Raj is followed by anarchism, and the answer to the others is that now there is no need for any government. This debate has taken place earlier. Even if we pay little attention to this or other such things, we shall have to agree that the people had agreed to a contract which the famous French thinker, Rousseau, called a social contract. According to the contract, a person would surrender a part of his freedom, a part of his income, in return for which he would be provided with security and peace. After all this, what is worth considering is whether this contract was fulfilled. After establishing the government, the State and the Church hatched a conspiracy. People were told that these persons, the rulers, had been sent by God (Theory of Divine Rights of Sovereignty). People were afraid of God and the king was able to carry out wilful oppression. The Tsar in Russia and King Louis in France are good examples to reveal the truth of this matter, because this conspiracy could not be carried out for too long; Pope Gregory and King Henry fell out with each other. The Pope incited the people against King Henry's rule and Henry shattered the bogey of religion. The meaning is that selfish people fought and these misconceptions were destroyed. Anyway, people rose in rebellion again and killed the cruel King Louis. The entire world was in a state of chaos. Democratic governments were established, but complete freedom was still not won. On the one side, the Austrian minister, Metternich was oppressing people and thus disillusioning them through autocratic royal rule, and on the other side in America, the poor slaves were in a miserable condition in a democracy. The French masses were struggling time and again to raise themselves from the morass of poverty. Even today, France is a democracy but people do not have complete freedom. That is the reason the anarchists say that no government is required. In every other thing, they are similar to the communists, but one or two things differ. The eminent communist Karl Marx's well-known friend Fredrick Engels has written about his own and Marx's Communism; and it is our ideal as well: 'Communism also looks forward to a period in the evolution of the society when the State will become superfluous and having no longer any function to perform, will die away.'

This means that political power should disappear and people should have a sense of fraternity. Italy's famous political thinker, Machiavelli believed that some form of rule should always prevail, whether it is a democracy or a monarchy. He believed in strong rule, like an iron fist. But the anarchists ask what is soft or hard. They want neither a soft nor a strong government. They say, "Undermine the whole conception of a State and then and then only we have liberty worth having." People would say that that is absurd; if there is no government, there would be no law, no police to enforce the law, and this would lead to chaos. But they say this view is also wrong. The famous political philosopher, Henry David Thoreau said, "Law never made a man whit more just, and by means of their respect for it even the well-disposed are daily made agents of injustice."

There doesn't seem to be any untruth in this. We can see that as law becomes more rigid, corruption also increases. It is an ordinary complaint that earlier without any written agreement, thousands of rupees would be exchanged and no one would cheat. Now, agreements have signatures, thumb impressions, witnesses, and are registered. But fraud is on the rise. Then the solution they suggest is that the needs of every person should be met, everything should go according to his wish, and there would be no sin or crime.'

"Crime is naught but misdirected energy. So long as every institution of today, economic, political, social and moral conspires to misdirect human energy into wrong channels, so long as most people are out of place doing the things they loathe to do, living a life they hate to live, crime will be inevitable and all the laws or the statutes can only increase but never do away with crime."

If a person has complete freedom, then he would be able to do things according to his own will. There would be no injustice. If the exploitation by the capitalists does not end, even the most stringent of laws would not help. People say that human nature is such that it cannot survive without some government. Human beings can cause a great deal of harm if they are not kept on a leash. Commenting on human nature in his book *The Principles of Politics*, the author A.R. Lord says that ants can live in a group, animals can live in a group, but not human beings. Man is greedy, inhuman and idle by nature. Hearing such talk, Emma Goldman lost her temper and in *Anarchism and Other Essays*, she wrote, 'Every fool from king to policeman, from a flat-headed person to the visionless dabbler in science presumes to speak authoritatively of human nature.' She says that the bigger a fool a person is, the more stridently his opinion in this matter is expressed. Have human beings ever been tested by giving them complete freedom, that one is forever crying over their flaws? She feels that small elected bodies should be made and the work should be carried out freely.

Private Property

The third most important thing is Private Property. In fact, it is the question of filling one's belly that makes the world goes around. It is for this that sermons preaching patience, contentment, etc., are crafted. Till now, everything in life was done for the sake of property; now, the anarchists, communists, socialists are all against property. As Emma Goldman says, "'Property is robbery' (Proudhon) but without risk or danger to the robber."

The notion of amassing property makes a person greedy. Then, he becomes increasingly more stony-hearted. Mercy and humanity begin to fade from his heart. A government is required for the security of property. This again leads to an escalation of greed and the ultimate end of that is—first, imperialism, and then, war, bloodshed and a lot of destruction. There would be no greed if everything becomes common property. Everyone would work together. There would be no fear of theft or robbery. There would be no need for the police, jail, court or army. And those with fat bellies and the parasites would also work. Production will be more even with fewer hours of work. People can have good education as well. There would be spontaneous peace and prosperity would increase. That is, they emphasize how very important it is to eradicate ignorance from the world.

In fact, property is the most important issue; that is why another essay is required to debate this issue. The real issue arises from bread; Karl Manning averred clearly, "Ask for work and if they don't give you work, ask for bread and if they do not give you work or bread, then take bread." Meaning that if one doesn't get either work or food, then steal food. What right does one have to gorge on cakes when others may not even get dry crumbs of bread? He also asked why a person born in a destitute household should be forced to scrimp and save, whereas a person born in a prosperous household should grow fat on idleness. The precept 'Let riches add to riches' should be stopped. It is for these reasons that they shattered the illusion of the sanctity of private property for the sake of the principle of equal opportunity. They say that property is attached to corruption, and law is needed to protect it which in turn requires a government. In fact, this is at the root of all evil. As soon as this is removed, everything will be all right. What do they really want; how will it really work? This is a vast question.

It has been stated above that anarchists are anti-God and religion because these cause mental slavery. Secondly, they are against the government, because this is physical slavery. They say that it is wrong to inspire human beings to do good by the lure of heaven or fear of hell, or by wielding the stick of law. And it is an insult to the nobility of man. One should attain knowledge freely and then work according to one's will and spend one's life happily. People say that this would mean that we wish to keep mankind in a state of wildness; as we were at the beginning. This is a false interpretation; in olden days, due to ignorance, people could not go far away. But now, with full awareness, establishing mutual relations in the world, man should live free. There should be no greed for money. And the issue of money should be eradicated.

In the next essay, we shall write about some other things regarding this philosophy, different viewpoints, history and the reasons for its unpopularity, and the reason for the inclusion of violence in this.

What Is Anarchism – III; 1928

In the previous two essays, we have presented the popular notions regarding anarchy. The curiosity of the public cannot be assuaged merely with these two essays about such an important topic that has recently emerged before the world as a reaction to the world's trite thoughts and traditions. Several doubts raise their heads. Even so, we are placing the broad principles before the readers so that they may understand the main ideas. Now, similarly, we shall write about the ideology of communism, socialism and nihilism, so that Hindustan becomes familiar with the ideologies currently prevalent in the world. But before writing about any other topic, the intention is to write down several important and interesting facts about anarchism, which also touches upon the history of nihilism; that is, what have the anarchists done so far? How did they acquire such an unsavoury reputation?

We have presented their thoughts above. Now, we want to discuss what they did to give a practical shape to their ideas and how they confronted very powerful governments with the use of force and even staked their lives in that conflict.

The fact is that when oppression and exploitation crosses a certain limit, when peaceful and free movement is crushed, then those who are always doers begin their work secretly and are ready to fight oppression as soon as they see it. When the poor working class was being exploited appallingly in Europe, all their efforts were crushed or were being crushed at that time, Mikhail Bakunin, who belonged to a prosperous family in Russia and was a top officer in an arms factory, was sent to Poland to deal with the revolt. There, the manner in which the rebels were being brutally crushed brought about a change in his mindset and he became a revolutionary. Ultimately, his thoughts turned towards anarchism. He resigned from his job in 1834. Subsequently, he reached Paris through Berlin and Switzerland. Those days, most of the governments were against him due to his views. Till 1864, he evolved his beliefs and propagated them among the working class.

Later, he gained control over the International Workingmen's Association and, from 1860 to 1870, he consolidated his group. On September 4, 1870, an announcement was made to establish a third Republic in Paris. There was unrest and riots in several places in France against the capitalist government. Bakunin was involved in these. They were the stronger side. But, in a few days, they lost and left the place.

In 1873, there was a revolt in Hispania. He joined in and fought. For some time, the matter was really hot, then it finally ended in a defeat. When they returned from there, a fight was raging in Italy. He went there and took the reins of the battle in his hands. After some initial differences, Garibaldi also joined him. After a few days of opposition, they lost there as well. In this manner, his entire life was spent waging battles. When he grew old, he wrote a letter to his compatriots saying that he would relinquish the leadership so that their work did not suffer. Finally, in 1876, he died due to an illness.

Later, four very strong people got ready for this task with great determination. They were Carlo Cafiero, an Italian belonging to quite a prosperous family. The second was Malatesta; he was a great doctor. But he renounced everything to become a revolutionary. The third was Paul Brousse, who was also a famous doctor. The fourth was Peter Kropotkin. He was from a Russian royal family. It was often said jokingly that he was to become the Tsar. They were all devotees of Bakunin. He said that they had propagated enough with the tongue, but it had had no effect. They were tired of hearing about new-fangled ideologies. These hadn't had any effect on the public. So, now it was time to propagate action. Kropotkin said, "A single deed makes more propaganda in a few days than a thousand pamphlets. The Government defends itself. It rages pitilessly, but, by this, it only caused further deeds to be committed by one or more persons and drives the insurgents to heroism. One deed brings forth another, opponents join the mutiny, the Government splits into factions, harshness intensifies the conflict, concessions come too late, the revolution breaks out."

Peter Kropotkin was one of the Russian revolutionaries. After being arrested, he was incarcerated in the Peter and Paul Fortress. He escaped from this very strongly-guarded prison and began to disseminate his ideas in Europe. These things tell us his state of mind in those days.

First of all, he celebrated the anniversary of the establishment of the rule of the workers in Berne city in France. This was the March 18, 1876. He took out a procession of workers on that day and got into a scuffle with the police in the streets. A riot ensued when policemen tried to uproot their red flag. Several policemen were seriously injured. In the end, all these people were arrested and sentenced for ten to forty days in jail.

In the month of April, they incited the peasants of Italy and set off riots in several parts of the country. Even there their companions were arrested, out of whom several were released. Now their strategy was a kind of publicity. That is why they used to say, "Neither money nor organizations nor literature was needed any longer (for their propaganda work). One human being in revolt with torch or dynamite was off to instruct the world."

From the next year onwards, in 1868, such activities were on the rise. An attempt was made to assassinate the Italian emperor Umberto when he was travelling in a motorcar with his daughter. Emperor Wilhelm I of Germany was shot at by an ordinary youth. After three weeks, Dr Karl Nobiling also tried to shoot at the Emperor from a window. In those days in Germany, the movements of the poor working classes were silenced brutally. After that, it was decided in a meeting that the corrupt capitalist class and the government, and the police that colluded with it, should be frightened in whatever way it was possible. On December 15, 1833, a notorious police officer by the name of Ulubek was killed in Willirid Floridsdorf. On June 23, 1884, Rouget was hanged for this crime. The very next day, Blatik, a police officer, was killed to avenge the hanging. The Austrian government was enraged, and in Vienna, the police besieged several people and arrested them; and two of them were hanged. There were strikes in Leon. One of the striking men, Fournier, shot his capitalist owner. He was awarded a pistol in a ceremony held to honour him. In 1888, there was a lot of unrest there and the silk workers were starving. At that time, the capitalist's newspaper-owning friends and other rich friends were busy living it up elsewhere. A bomb was thrown there. The rich were terrified. Sixty anarchists were held. Only three were acquitted. But still, the search for the actual bomb thrower did not come to an end. He was finally caught and hanged. And, in this way, this line of thinking gained momentum. And then, wherever there were strikes, murders would take place. The anarchists were blamed for all this, and as a result, people would shudder at the very mention of them.

A German anarchist, Johann Most, who worked in an office, went to America in 1882. He also began to place his ideas before the people. He was a very good orator and impressed his audience in America. In 1886, several strikes were called in Chicago and other places. In one paper factory, an anarchist called Spies was giving a speech. The owners tried to shut the factory; a riot erupted. The police were called in and they began firing as soon as they came. Six men were killed and several were injured. Spies were furious. He himself composed a notice and decreed that the workers should unite to avenge the murder of their innocent comrades. The next day, on May 4, 1886, the Hay Market procession was to be taken out. The President of the city had come to watch it. He saw nothing objectionable going on. So, he went there. Later, the police came and without any provocation, began to beat up people and asked them to stop the procession. Just then a bomb was thrown at the police and many policemen were killed. Several people were arrested and hanged. As he was leaving, one of them said, 'I repeat, I am a sworn enemy of this present state of affairs. I want this political establishment to be destroyed and we should be able to wield political power ourselves. You may laugh that I shall no longer be able to throw bombs, but let me tell you that your oppression has forced every worker to handle and throw a bomb. You should know that after I am hanged, another one will be born. I see you with revulsion in my eyes and want to trample your State. Hang me.' Anyway, several such incidents happened. But there are a couple of other famous incidents. The American President, McKinley was shot at and then there was a strike in Carnegie steel company. The workers were being brutalized here. The owner, Henry C. Frick, was injured by an anarchist, Alexander, who was sentenced for life. Anyway, this is how anarchism spread to America and began to be practiced.

In Europe, too, things were bad. The anarchists' feud with the police and the government had intensified. Finally, a youth named Vaillant threw a bomb in the Assembly, but a woman caught his hand and stopped him; as a result of which nothing much happened, except that some deputies were injured. He offered an explanation in a ringing voice, "It takes a loud voice to make the deaf hear. Now you will punish me, but I have no fear because I have struck at your hearts. You, who oppress the poor and those who work hard, starve, and whose blood you suck and take pleasure in it. I have hurt you. Now it is your turn."

Several appeals were made on his behalf. Even the most seriously injured member of the Assembly requested the jury to show mercy to him, but the jury, presided over by a person named Carnot, refused to pay any attention and sentenced him to death by hanging. Later, an Italian boy stabbed Carnot with a knife with the name Vaillant written on it.

In this manner, unable to endure any more oppression, bombs were set off even in Spain and finally an Italian killed a minister. In a similar manner, the Emperor of Greece and the Empress of Austria were also attacked. In 1900, Gaetano Bresci killed the Emperor of Italy, Umberto. In this manner, these people smilingly gave up their lives for the sake of the poor ... kissed the gallows joyfully. That is why, even those opposed to them could do nothing against them. Their last martyrs, Sacco and Vanzetti, have been hanged only last year. The courage with which these people went to the gallows is known to everyone.

And this is the brief history of anarchism and its activities. Next time, we shall write an essay about Communism.

10

'Beware, Ye Tyrants; Beware'
(December, 1928)

A handwritten leaflet written on December 18, 1928, on Mozang House den explaining the reasons for British officer J.P. Saunders' murder and pasted on several walls of Lahore in the night between the 18th and 19th. A copy in Bhagat Singh's handwriting was produced as an exhibit in the Lahore Conspiracy Case.

POSTER AFTER SAUNDERS' MURDER
"Notice"
By Hindustan Socialist Republican Army.
'Beware, Ye Tyrants; Beware'

J.P. Saunders is dead; Lala Lajpat Rai is avenged!

Really it is horrible to imagine that so lowly and violent hand of an ordinary police official, J.P. Saunders, could ever dare to touch in such an insulting way the body of one so old, so revered and so loved by 300 millions of people of Hindustan and thus cause his death. The youth and manhood of India was challenged by blows hurled down on the head of the India's nationhood. And let the world know that India still lives; that the blood of youths has not been totally cooled down and that they can still risk their lives, if the honour of their nation is at stake. And it is proved through this act by those obscure who are ever persecuted, condemned and denounced even by their own people.

Beware, Ye Tyrants; Beware.

Do not injure the feelings of a downtrodden and oppressed country. Think twice before perpetrating such a diabolical deed, and remember that despite 'Arms Act' and strict guards against the smuggling of arms, the revolvers will ever continue to flow in—if no sufficient at present for and armed revolt, then at least sufficient to avenge the national insults. In spite of all the denunciations and condemnation of their own kiths and kins, and ruthless repression and persecution of the alien government, party of young men will ever live to teach a lesson to the haughty rulers. They will be so bold as to cry even amidst the raging storm of opposition and repression, even on the scaffold:

"LONG LIVE THE REVOLUTION!"

Sorry for the death of a man. But in this man has died the representative of an institution which is so cruel, lowly, and so base that it must be abolished. In this man has died an agent of the British authority in India—the most tyrannical of government of the governments in the world.

Sorry for the bloodshed of a human being; but the sacrifice of individuals at the altar of the revolution that will bring freedom to all and make the exploitation of man by man impossible, is inevitable.

"Long Live The Revolution!"

Signed,
Balraj
December 18, 1928

11

"It Takes a Loud Voice to Make the Deaf Hear!"

(April, 1929)

On April 8, 1929, Bhagat Singh and Batukeshwar Dutt, on behalf of Hindustan Socialist Republican Association, delivered a strong message of dissent in the Central Assembly Hall, Delhi during the enactment of Public Safety and Trade Disputes Bills by Viceroy Lord Irwin. Even though the majority of members were opposed to both the bills and had rejected them earlier, the Viceroy was about to make a proclamation on their enactment.

Inspired by a French anarchist martyr Auguste Valliant—known for a similar attack on the French Parliament in 1893—Bhagat Singh and Batukeshwar Dutt threw non-lethal bombs in the corridors of the Assembly Hall along with several copies of this sharply-worded leaflet in order to make the 'deaf hear'; their slogans of *'Inqilab Zindabad!'* (Long Live Revolution!) and *'Samrajyawad ka nash ho!'* (Down with Imperialism!) reverberating in the hall.

THE HINDUSTAN SOCIALIST REPUBLICAN ARMY (NOTICE)

"It takes a loud voice to make the deaf hear", with these immortal words uttered on a similar occasion by Valiant, a French anarchist martyr, do we strongly justify this action of ours.

Without repeating the humiliating history of the past 10 years of the working of the reforms (Montagu-Chelmsford Reforms) and without mentioning the insults hurled at the Indian nation through this House the so-called Indian Parliament—we want to point out that, while the people expecting some more crumbs of reforms from the Simon Commission, and are ever quarrelling over the distribution of the expected bones, the government is thrusting upon us new repressive measures like the Public Safety and the Trade Disputes Bill, while reserving the Press Sedition Bill for the next session. The indiscriminate arrests of labour leaders working in the open field clearly indicate whither the wind blows.

In these extremely provocative circumstances, the Hindustan Socialist Republican Association, in all seriousness, realizing their full responsibility, had decided and ordered its army to do this particular action, so that a stop be put to this humiliating farce and to let the alien bureaucratic exploiters do what they wish, but they must be made to come before the public eve in their naked form.

Let the representatives of the people return to their constituencies and prepare the masses for the coming revolution, and let the government know that while protesting against the Public Safety and Trade Disputes Bills and the callous murder of Lala Lajpat Rai, on behalf of the helpless Indian masses, we want to emphasize the lesson often repeated by history, that it is easy to kill individuals but you cannot kill the ideas. Great empires crumbled while the ideas survived, Bourbons and Czars fell, while the revolution marched ahead triumphantly.

We are sorry to admit that we who attach so great a sanctity to human life, who dream of a glorious future, when man will be enjoying perfect peace and full liberty, have been forced to shed human blood. But the sacrifice of individuals at the altar of the 'Great Revolution' that will bring freedom to all, rendering the exploitation of man by man impossible, is inevitable.

"Long Live the Revolution!" [B]

Signed,
Balraj [C]
Commander-in-Chief

Transcriber's Notes

[A.] This document was primarily written by Bhagat Singh. On April 8, 1929, Bhagat Singh and Batukeshwar Dutt showered copies of the leaflet on the floor of Central Assembly Hall in New Delhi after tossing two non-lethal bombs into the Assembly Hall corridors.

[B.] This phrase (translated from *"Inquilab Zindabad!"*) became one of the most enduring slogans of the Indian independence movement. Bhagat Singh and Batukeshwar Dutta repeated the slogan at their June 1929 trial on charges related to the bomb-throwing incident.

[C.] "Balraj" was the pen name for the Commander-in-Chief of the Hindustan Socialist Republican Army, Chandra Shekhar Azad.

12

"Do Away with the Fear of Doing Radical Things"
Bhagat Singh Wrote to Sukhdev
(April, 1929)

This letter deals with the views of Bhagat Singh on the question of love and sacrifice in the life of a revolutionary. It was written on April 5, 1929 in Sita Ram Bazar House, Delhi. The letter was taken to Lahore by Shri Shiv Verma and handed over to Sukhdev. It was later recovered from him at the time of his arrest on April 13 and was produced as one of the exhibits in Lahore Conspiracy Case.

Dear Brother,

By the time you receive this letter, I will be gone to a far off destination. Let me assure you that I am prepared for the voyage in spite of all the sweet memories and charms of my life here. Up to this day, one thing pinched in my heart and it was this that my brother, my own brother, misunderstood and accused me of a very serious charge—the charge of weakness. Today, I am quite satisfied. Today, more than ever do I feel that it was nothing but a misunderstanding, a wrong calculation. My overfrankness was interpreted as my talkativeness, and my confession as my weakness. And now I feel it was misunderstanding and only misunderstanding. I am not weak, not weaker than anyone amongst us, brother. With a clear heart I go, will you clear your heart, too? It will be very kind of you. But note that you are to take no hasty step, soberly and calmly you are to carry on the work. Don't try to take the chance at the very outset. You have some duty towards the public, and that you can fulfill by continuing this work. As a suggestion I would say that M.R. Shastri appeals to me more than ever. Try to bring him in the arena, provided he himself may be willing, clearly knowing the dark future. Let him mix with men and study their psychology. If he will work in the right spirit, he will be the better judge. Arrange as you may deem fit. Now, brother, let us be happy.

By the way, I am saying that I cannot help arguing once again my case in the matter under discussion. Again, do I emphasize that I am full of ambition and hope and of full charm of life. But I can renounce all at the time of need, and that is the real sacrifice. These things can never be hindrance in the way of man, provided he be a man. You will have the practical proof in the near future. While discussing anybody's character you asked me one thing, whether love ever proved helpful to any man. Yes, I answer that question today. To Mazzini it was. You must have read that after the utter failure and crushing defeat of his first rising, he could not bear the misery and haunting ideas of his dead comrades. He would have gone mad or committed suicide, but for one letter of a girl he loved. He would have been as strong as any one, nay stronger than all.

As regards the moral status of love I may say that it in itself is nothing but passion, not an animal passion but a human one, and very sweet, too. Love, in itself, can never be an animal passion. Love always elevates the character of man. It never lowers him, provided love be love. You can't call these girls—mad people, as we generally see in films—lovers. They always play in the hands of animal's passions. The true love cannot be created. It comes of its own accord;

nobody can say when. It is but natural. And I may tell you that a young man and a young girl can love each other, and with the aid of their love they can overcome the passions themselves and can maintain their purity.

I may clear one thing here; when I said that love has human weakness, I did not say it for an ordinary human being at this stage, where the people generally are. But that is most idealistic stage when man would overcome all these sentiments, the love, the hatred, and so on. When man will take reason as the sole basis of his activity. But at present it is not bad, rather good and useful to man. And, moreover, while rebuking the love. I rebuked the love of one individual for one, and that, too, in idealistic stage. And even then, man must have the strongest feelings of love which he may not confine to one individual and may make it universal. Now, I think I have cleared my position.

One thing I may tell you to mark; we—in spite of all radical ideas that we cherish—have not been able to do away with the over idealistic Arya Samajist conception of morality. We may talk glibly about all the radical things that can possibly be conceived, but in practical life we begin to tremble at the very outset. This I will request you do away with. And may I, without fear at all the misapprehensions in my mind, request you do kindly lower the standard of your over-idealism a bit, not to be harsh to those who will live behind and be the victims of a disease as myself? Don't rebuke them and thus add to their woes and miseries. They need your sympathy. May I repeat that you, without bearing any sort of grudge against any particular individual, will sympathize with those who needed the most? But you cannot realize these things unless and until you yourself fall a victim to this. But, why I am writing all this? I wanted to be frank. I have cleared my heart.

Wish you all success and happy life.

Yours,
B. S.

13

Joint Statement: Full Text of Statement of Bhagat Singh and B.K. Dutt Regarding the Assembly Bomb Case (June, 1929)

On April 29, 1929, Bhagat Singh, along with his HSRA comrade Batukeshwar Dutt, threw non-lethal bombs in the Central Assembly Hall, Delhi, protesting the enactment of Public Safety and Trade Disputes Bills by Viceroy Lord Irwin. With the slogans of *'Inquilab Zindabad!*(Long Live Revolution!)' and 'Down with Imperialism!' reverberating in the assembly hall, the two revolutionaries threw the bombs to "make the deaf hear".

This statement was read in the Court on June 6, 1929, by Mr. Asaf Ali on behalf of Bhagat Singh and B.K. Dutt.

We stand charged with certain serious offences, and at this stage it is only right that we must explain our conduct.

In this connection, the following questions arise:

1. Were the bombs thrown into Chamber, and, if so, why?
2. Is the charge, as framed by the Lower Court, correct or otherwise?

To the first half of first question, our reply is in the affirmative, but since some of the so-called 'eye witnesses' have perjured themselves and since we are not denying our liability to that extent, let our statement about them be judged for what it is worth. By way of an illustration, we may point out that the evidence of Sergeant Terry regarding the seizure of the pistol from one of us is a deliberate falsehood, for neither of us had the pistol at the time we gave ourselves up. Other witnesses, too, who have deposed to having seen bombs being thrown by us have not scrupled to tell lies. This fact had its own moral for those who aim at judicial purity and fair play. At the same time, we acknowledge the fairness of the Public Prosecutor and the judicial attitude of the Court so far.

Viceroy's Views Endorsed

In our reply to the next half of the first question, we are constrained to go into some detail to offer a full and frank explanation of our motive and the circumstances leading up to what has now become a historic event.

When we were told by some of the police officers, who visited us in jail, that Lord Irwin—in his address to the joint session of the two houses—described the event as an attack directed against no individual but against an institution itself, we readily recognized that the true significance of the incident had been correctly appreciated. We are next to none in our love for humanity. Far from having any malice against any individual, we hold human life sacred beyond words. We are neither perpetrators of dastardly outrages, and, therefore, a disgrace to the country, as the pseudo-socialist Dewan. Chaman Lal is reported to have described us, nor are we 'lunatics' as *The Tribune* of Lahore and some others would have it believed.

Practical Protest

We humbly claim to be no more than serious students of the history and conditions of our country and her aspirations. We despise hypocrisy. Our practical protest was against the institution, which, since its birth, has eminently helped to display not only its worthlessness but its far-reaching power for mischief. We have been convinced that it exists only to demonstrate to the world an Indian's humiliation and helplessness, and it symbolizes the overriding domination of an irresponsible and autocratic rule. Time and again the national demand has been pressed by people's representatives only to find the waste paper basket as its final destination.

Attack on Institution

Solemn resolutions passed by the House have been contemptuously trampled underfoot on the floor of the so-called Indian parliament. Resolution regarding the repeal of the repressive and arbitrary measures have been treated with sublime contempt, and the government measures and proposals, rejected as unacceptable buy the elected members of the legislatures, have been restored by mere stroke of the pen. In short, we have utterly failed to find any justification for the existence of an institution which, despite all its pomp and splendour, organized with the hard-earned money of the sweating millions of India, is only a hollow show and a mischievous make-believe. Alike, have we failed to comprehend the mentality of the public leaders who help the government to squander public time and money on such a manifestly stage-managed exhibition of Indian's helpless subjection.

No Hope for Labour

We have been ruminating upon all these matters, as also upon the wholesale arrests of the leaders of the labour movement. When the introduction of the Trade Disputes Bill brought us into the Assembly to watch its progress, the course of the debate only served to confirm our conviction that the labouring millions of India had nothing to expect from an institution that stood as a menacing monument to the strangling of the exploiters and the serfdom of the helpless labourers.

Finally, the insult of what we consider, an inhuman and barbarous measure was hurled on the devoted head of the representatives of the entire country, and the starving and struggling millions were deprived of their primary right and the sole means of improving their economic welfare. None who has felt like us for the dumb-driven drudges of labourers could possibly witness this spectacle with equanimity. None whose heart bleeds for them, who have given their life-blood in silence to the building up of the economic structure could repress the cry which this ruthless blow had wrung out of our hearts.

Bomb Needed

Consequently, bearing in mind the words of the late Mr. S.R. Das, once Law Member of the Governor—General's Executive Council, which appeared in the famous letter he had addressed to his son, to the effect that the 'Bomb was necessary to awaken England from her dreams', we dropped the bomb on the floor of the Assembly Chamber to register our protest on behalf of those who had no other means left to give expression to their heart-rending agony. Our sole purpose was "to make the deaf hear" and to give the heedless a timely warning. Others have as keenly felt as we have done, and from under the seeming stillness of the sea of Indian humanity, a veritable storm is about to break out. We have only hoisted the "danger-signal" to warn those who are speeding along without heeding the grave dangers ahead. We have only marked the end of an era of Utopian non-violence, of whose futility the rising generation has been convinced beyond the shadow of doubt.

Ideal Explained

We have used the expression Utopian non-violence, in the foregoing paragraph which requires some explanation. Force when aggressively applied is "violence" and is, therefore, morally unjustifiable, but when it is used in the furtherance of a legitimate cause, it has its moral justification. The elimination of force at all costs in Utopian, and the mew movement which has arisen in the country, and of that dawn we have given a warning, is inspired by the ideal which guided Guru Gobind Singh and Shivaji, Kamal Pasha and Riza Khan, Washington and Garibaldi, Lafayette and Lenin.

As both the alien government and the Indian public leaders appeared to have shut their eyes to the existence of this movement, we felt it as our duty to sound a warning where it could not go unheard. We have so far dealt with the motive behind the incident in question, and now we must define the extent of our intention.

No Personal Grudge

We bore no personal grudge or malice against anyone of those who received slight injuries or against any other person in the Assembly. On the contrary, we repeat that we hold human life sacred beyond words, and would sooner lay down our own lives in the service of humanity than injure anyone else. Unlike the mercenary soldiers of the imperialist armies who are disciplined to kill without compunction, we respect, and, in so far as it lies in our power, we attempt to save human life. And still we admit having deliberately thrown the bombs into the Assembly Chamber. Facts, however, speak for themselves and our intention would be judged from the result of the action without bringing in Utopian hypothetical circumstances and presumptions.

No Miracle

Despite the evidence of the government expert, the bombs that were thrown in the Assembly Chamber resulted in slight damage to an empty bench and some slight abrasions in less than half a dozen cases, while government scientists and experts have ascribed this result to a miracle, we see nothing but a precisely scientific process in all this incident. Firstly, the two bombs exploded in vacant spaces within the wooden barriers of the desks and benches, secondly, even those who were within two feet of the explosion, for instance, Mr. P. Rau, Mr. Shanker Rao, and Sir George Schuster were either not hurt or only slightly scratched. Bombs of the capacity deposed to by the government expert (though his estimate, being imaginary is exaggerated), loaded with an effective charge of potassium chlorate and sensitive (explosive) picrate would have smashed the barriers and laid many low within some yards of the explosion.

Again, had they been loaded with some other high explosive, with a charge of destructive pellets or darts, they would have sufficed to wipe out a majority of the Members of the Legislative Assembly. Still again, we could have flung them into the official box which was occupied by some notable persons. And finally we could have ambushed Sir

John Simon whose luckless Commission was loathed by all responsible people and who was sitting in the President's gallery at the time. All these things, however, were beyond our intention and bombs did no more than they were designed to do, and the miracle consisted in no more than the deliberate aim which landed them in safe places.

We then deliberately offered ourselves to bear the penalty for what we had done and to let the imperialist exploiters know that by crushing individuals, they cannot kill ideas. By crushing two insignificant units, a nation cannot be crushed. We wanted to emphasize the historical lesson that *lettres de cachets* and Bastilles could not crush the revolutionary movement in France. Gallows and the Siberian mines could not extinguish the Russian Revolution. Bloody Sunday, and Black and Tans failed to strangle the movement of Irish freedom. Can ordinances and Safety Bills snuff out the flames of freedom in India? Conspiracy cases, trumped up or discovered and the incarceration of all young men, who cherish the vision of a great ideal, cannot check the march of revolution. But a timely warning, if not unheeded, can help to prevent loss of life and general sufferings. We took it upon ourselves to provide this warning and our duty is done.

Bhagat Singh was asked in the lower court what he meant by word "Revolution". In answer to that question, he said: "Revolution" does not necessarily involve sanguinary strife nor is there any place in it for individual vendetta. It is not the cult of the bomb and the pistol. By "Revolution", we mean that the present order of things, which is based on manifest injustice, must change. Producers or labourers in spite of being the most necessary element of society, are robbed of the fruits of their labour and deprived of their elementary rights by their exploiters. The peasant who grows corn for all, starves with his family, the weaver who supplies the world market with textile fabrics, has not enough to cover his own and his children's bodies, masons, smiths and carpenters who raise magnificent palaces, live like pariahs in the slums. The capitalists and exploiters, the parasites of society, squander millions on their whims. These terrible inequalities and forced disparity of chances are bound to lead to chaos. This state of affairs cannot last long, and it is obvious, that the present order of society in merry-making is on the brink of a volcano.

The whole edifice of this civilization, if not saved in time, shall crumble. A radical change, therefore, is necessary and it is the duty of those who realize it to reorganize society on the socialistic basis. Unless this thing is done and the exploitation of man by man and of nations by nations is brought to an end, sufferings and carnage with which humanity is threatened today cannot be prevented. All talk of ending war and ushering in an era of universal peace is undisguised hypocrisy.

By "Revolution", we mean the ultimate establishment of an order of society which may not be threatened by such breakdown, and in which the sovereignty of the proletariat should be recognized and a world federation should redeem humanity from the bondage of capitalism and misery of imperial wars.

This is our ideal, and with this ideology as our inspiration, we have given a fair and loud enough warning.

If, however, it goes unheeded and the present system of government continues to be an impediment in the way of the natural forces that are swelling up, a grim struggle will ensure involving the overthrow of all obstacles, and the establishment of the dictatorship of the proletariat to pave the way for the consummation of the ideal of revolution. Revolution is an inalienable right of mankind. Freedom is an imperishable birthright of all. Labour is the real sustainer of society. The sovereignty of the ultimate destiny of the workers.

For these ideals, and for this faith, we shall welcome any suffering to which we may be condemned. At the altar of this revolution we have brought our youth as an incense, for no sacrifice is too great for so magnificent a cause. We are content, we await the advent of Revolution.

Long Live Revolution!

14

Hunger-Strikers' Demand
(June, 1929)

Bhagat Singh and B.K. Dutt were sentenced to transportation for life in the Delhi Assembly Bomb Case. After conviction, they were transferred to Mianwali and Lahore jails respectively. They started hunger strike in order to ensure better treatment to political prisoners in jails. After a few days, Bhagat Singh was also shifted from Mianwali to Lahore Central Prison. Dutt was already there. They jointly addressed this letter to the Home Member, Government of India, enumerating their demands. From here on, started a period of prolonged struggle to ensure political prisoners receive better treatment.

Central Jail, Lahore, 24.6.29

We, Bhagat Singh and B. K. Dutt, were sentenced to life transportation in the Assembly Bomb Case, Delhi the April 19, 1929. As long as we were under trial prisoners in Delhi Jail, we were accorded a very good treatment from that jail to the Mianwali and Lahore Central Jails respectively. We wrote an application to the higher authorities asking for better diet and a few other facilities, and refused to take the jail diet.

Our demands were as follows:

We, as political prisoners, should be given better diet and the standard of our diet should at least be the same as that of European prisoners. (It is not the sameness of dietary that we demand, but the sameness of standard of diet.)

We shall not be forced to do any hard and undignified labours at all.

All books, other than those proscribed, along with writing materials, should be allowed to us without any restriction.

At least one standard daily paper should be supplied to every political prisoner.

Political prisoners should have a special ward of their own in every jail, provided with all necessities as those of the Europeans. And all the political prisoners in one jail must be kept together in that ward.

Toilet necessities should be supplied.

Better clothing.

We have explained above the demands that we made. They are the most reasonable demands. The Jail authorities told us one day that the higher authorities have refused to comply with our demands.

Apart from that, they handle us very roughly while feeding us artificially, and Bhagat Singh was lying quite senseless on the June 10, 1929, for about 15 minutes, after the forcible feeding, which we request to be stopped without any further delay.

In addition, we may be permitted to refer to the recommendations made in the U.P. Jail Committee by Pt. Jagat Narain and K.B. Hafiz Hidayat Hussain. They have recommended the political prisoners to be treated as "better class prisoners."

We request you to kindly consider our demands at your earliest convenience.

By "political prisoners", we mean all those who are convicted for offences against the State. For instance, the people who were convicted in the Lahore Conspiracy cases, 1915-17, the Kakori Conspiracy cases, and sedition cases in general.

Yours,
Bhagat Singh
B. K. Dutt

15

Message to Punjab Students' Conference
(October, 1929)

The Second Punjab Students' Conference was held at Lahore on October 19, 1929, under the presidency of Netaji Subhash Chandra Bose. Bhagat Singh grabbed the opportunity and sent this message asking the students to plunge wholeheartedly into the upcoming movement of 1930-31 and pass on the message of revolution to the remotest corners of the country. It was jointly signed with his revolutionary compatriot B. K. Dutt. The message was read in an open session and received a thunderous applause from the students with the slogans of *'Bhagat Singh Zindabad!'* This shows how Bhagat Singh was able to inspire youth with his words and actions.

Comrades,

Today, we cannot ask the youth to take to pistols and bombs. Today, students are confronted with a far more important assignment. In the coming Lahore Session, the Congress is to give a call for a fierce fight for the independence of the country. The youth will have to bear a great burden in this difficult times in the history of the nation. It is true that students have faced death at the forward positions of the struggle for independence. Will they hesitate this time in proving their same staunchness and self-confidence? The youth will have to spread this revolutionary message to the far corner of the country. They have to awaken crores of slum dwellers of the industrial areas and villagers living in worn-out cottages, so that we will be independent and the exploitation of man by man will become an impossibility. Punjab is considered politically backward even otherwise. This is also the responsibility of the youth. Taking inspiration from the martyr Yatindra

Nath Das and with boundless reverence for the country, they must prove that they can fight with steadfast resolve in this struggle for independence.

16

On the Slogan of 'Long Live Revolution!'

(December, 1929)

Ramananda Chatterjee, the founder and editor of Calcutta-based monthly magazine Modern Review, ridiculed the slogan of 'Long Live Revolution!' through an editorial note calling it a "ceaseless revolutionary process" and presented an entirely wrong interpretation. Bhagat Singh wrote a reply and handed it over to the trying magistrate to be sent to the *Modern Review*. This response was published in *The Tribune* of December 24, 1929.

To,
The Editor
Modern Review,

You have in the December (1929) issue of your esteemed magazine, written a note under the caption "Long Live Revolution" and have pointed out the meaninglessness of this phrase. It would be impertinent on our part to try to refute or contradict the statement of such an old, experienced and renowned journalist as your noble self, for whom every enlightened Indian has profound admiration. Still we feel it our duty to explain what we desire to convey by the said phrase, as in a way it fell to our lot to give these "cries" a publicity in this country at this stage.

We are not the originators of this cry. The same cry had been used in Russian revolutionary movement. Upton Sinclair, the well-known socialist writer, has, in his recent novels *Boston* and *Oil!*, used this cry through some of the anarchist revolutionary characters. The phrase never means that the sanguinary strife should ever continue, or that nothing should ever be stationary even for a short while. By long usage this cry achieves a significance which may not be quite justifiable from the grammatical or the etymological point of view, but nevertheless we cannot abstract from that the association of ideas connected with that. All such shouts denote a general sense which is partly acquired and partly inherent in them. For instance, when we shout "Long Live Jatin Das!", we cannot and do not mean thereby that Das should physically be alive. What we mean by that shout is that the noble ideal of his life, the indomitable spirit which enabled that great martyr to bear such untold suffering and to make the extreme sacrifice for that we may show the same unfailing courage in pursuance of our ideal. It is that spirit that we allude to.

Similarly, one should not interpret the word "Revolution" in its literal sense. Various meanings and significances are attributed to this word, according to the interests of those who use or misuse it. For the established agencies of exploitation, it conjures up a feeling of blood-stained horror. To the revolutionaries, it is a sacred phrase. We tried to clear in our statement before the Session Judge, Delhi, in our trial in the Assembly Bomb Case, what we mean by the word "Revolution".

We stated therein that revolution did not necessarily involve sanguinary strife. It was not a cult of bomb and pistol. They may sometimes be mere means for its achievement. No doubt they play a prominent part in some movements, but they do not—for that very reason—become one and the same thing. A rebellion is not a revolution. It may ultimately lead to that end. The sense in which the word "Revolution" is used in that phrase, is the spirit, the longing for a change for the better. The people generally get accustomed to the established order of things and begin to tremble at the very idea of a change. It is this lethargical spirit that needs be replaced by the revolutionary spirit. Otherwise, degeneration gains the upper hand and the whole humanity is led astray by the reactionary forces. Such a state of affairs leads to stagnation and paralysis in human progress. The spirit of revolution should always permeate the soul of humanity, so that the reactionary forces may not accumulate (strength) to check its eternal onward march. Old order should change, always and ever, yielding place to new, so that one "good" order may not corrupt the world. It is, in this sense, that we raise the shout "Long Live Revolution!"

Yours sincerely,
Bhagat Singh
B. K. Dutt

17

Why I Am an Atheist
(October 1930)

This essay was originally written in English by Bhagat Singh in October 1930 while he was in Lahore Central Jail. It was written in order to document his thoughts on his religious friend Baba Randhir Singh's claim that Bhagat Singh became an atheist out of sheer vanity. Baba Randhir Singh, a freedom fighter, was in Lahore Central Jail in 1930-31. Being a God-fearing religious man, it pained him to learn that Bhagat Singh was a non-believer. He somehow managed to see Bhagat Singh in the condemned cell and tried to convince him about the existence of God, but failed. Baba lost his temper and tauntingly said: "You are giddy with fame and have developed an ego which is standing like a black curtain between you and the God." It was in reply to that remark that Bhagat Singh wrote this essay.

A new question has cropped up. Is it due to vanity that I do not believe in the existence of an omnipotent, omnipresent, and omniscient God? I had never imagined that I would ever have to confront such a question. But conversation with some friends has given me a hint that certain of my friends—if I am not claiming too much in thinking them to be so—are inclined to conclude from the brief contact they have had with me, that it was too much on my part to deny the existence of God and that there was a certain amount of vanity that actuated my disbelief. Well, the problem is a serious one. I do not boast to be quite above these human traits. I am a man and nothing more. None can claim to be more. I also have this weakness in me. Vanity does form a part of my nature. Amongst my comrades, I was called an autocrat. Even my friend Mr. B.K. Dutt sometimes called me so. On certain occasions I was decried as a despot. Some friends do complain, and very seriously too, that I involuntarily thrust my opinions upon others and get my proposals accepted. That this is true up to a certain extent, I do not deny. This may amount to egotism. There is vanity in me in as much as our cult as opposed to other popular creeds is concerned. But that is not personal. It may be, it is only legitimate pride in our cult and does not amount to vanity. Vanity, or to be more precise *"ahankar"*, is the excess of undue pride in one's self. Whether it is such an undue pride that has led me to atheism or whether it is after very careful study of the subject and after much consideration that I have come to disbelieve in God, is a question that I intend to discuss here. Let me first make it clear that egotism and vanity are two different things.

In the first place, I have altogether failed to comprehend as to how undue pride or vain gloriousness could ever stand in the way of a man in believing in God. I can refuse to recognize the greatness of a really great man, provided I have also achieved a certain amount of popularity without deserving it or without having possessed the qualities really essential or indispensable for the same purpose. That much is conceivable. But in what way can a man believing in God cease believing due to his personal vanity? There are only two ways. The man should either begin to think of himself a rival of God or he may begin to believe himself to be God. In neither case, can he become a genuine atheist. In the first case, he does not even deny the existence of his rival. In the second case as well, he admits the existence of a conscious being behind the screen guiding all the movements of nature. It is of no importance to us whether he thinks himself to be that Supreme Being or whether he thinks the supreme conscious being to be somebody apart from himself. The fundamental is there. His belief is there. He is by means an atheist. Well, here I am. I neither belong to the first category nor to the second. I deny the very existence of that Almighty Supreme Being. Why I deny it, shall be dealt with later on.

Here I want to clear one thing, that it is not vanity that has actuated me to adopt the doctrines of atheism. I am neither a rival nor an incarnation, nor the Supreme Being himself. One point is decided, that it is not vanity that has led me to this mode of thinking. Let me examine the facts to disprove this allegation. According to these friends of mine, I have grown vainglorious perhaps due to the undue popularity gained during the trials—both Delhi Bomb and Lahore Conspiracy cases. Well, let us see if their premises are correct. My atheism is not of so recent origin. I had stopped believing in God when I was an obscure young man, of whose existence my above-mentioned friends were not even aware. At least a college student cannot cherish any short of undue pride which may lead him to atheism. Though a favourite with some professors, and disliked by certain others. I was never an industrious or a studious boy. I could not get any chance of indulging in such feelings as vanity. I was rather a boy with a very shy nature, who had certain pessimistic dispositions about the future career. And in those days, I was not a perfect atheist. My grandfather under whose influence I was brought up is an orthodox Arya Samajist. An Arya Samajist is anything but an atheist. After finishing my primary education, I joined the D.A.V. School of Lahore and stayed in its boarding house for full one year. There, apart from morning and evening prayers, I used to recite *"The Gayatri Mantra"* for hours and hours. I was perfect devotee in those days. Later on, I began to live with my father. He is a liberal in as much as the orthodoxy of religions is concerned. It was through his teachings that I aspired to devote my life to the cause of freedom. But he is not an atheist. He is a firm believer. He used to encourage me for offering prayers daily. So, this is how I was brought up.

In the non-cooperation days I joined the National College. It was there that I began to think liberally and discuss and criticize all the religious problem, even about God. But still I was a devout believer. By that time, I had begun to preserve the unshorn and unclipped long hair but I could never believe in the mythology and doctrines of Sikhism or any other religion. But I had a firm faith in God's existence.

Later on I joined the revolutionary party. The first leader with whom I came in contact, though not convinced, could not dare to deny the existence of God. On my persistent inquiries about God, he used to say: "Pray whenever you want to." Now this is atheism less courage required for the adoption of that creed. The second leader with whom I came in contact was a firm believer. Let me mention his name-respected Comrade Sachindra Nath Sanyal, now undergoing life transportation in connection with the Kakori Conspiracy case. From the very first page of his famous and only book, *Bandi Jeevan: A Life in Chains* (or Incarcerated Life), the Glory of God is sung vehemently. On the last page of the second part of that beautiful book, his mystic—because of vedantism—praises showered upon God form a very conspicuous part of his thoughts. "The Revolutionary" distributed throughout India on January 28th, 1925, was according to the prosecution story the result of his intellectual labour. Now, as is inevitable in the secret work the prominent leader expresses his own views which are very dear to his person, and the rest of the workers have to acquiesce in them, in spite of differences which they might have. In that leaflet, one full paragraph was devoted to praise the Almighty and His rejoicings and doing. That is all mysticism. What I wanted to point out was that the idea of disbelief had not even germinated in the revolutionary party. The famous Kakori martyrs—all four of them—passed their last days in prayers. Ram Prasad Bismil was an orthodox Arya Samajist. Despite his wide studies in the field of socialism and communism, Rajen Lahiri could not suppress his desire of reciting hymns of the Upanishads and *The Gita*. I saw only one man amongst them, who never prayed and used to say: "Philosophy is the outcome of human weakness or limitation of knowledge." He is also undergoing a sentence of transportation for life. But he also never dared to deny the existence of God.

Up to that period, I was only a romantic idealist revolutionary. Up till then we were to follow. Now, came the time to shoulder the whole responsibility. Due to the inevitable reaction for some time the very existence of the party seemed impossible. Enthusiastic comrades—nay, leaders—began to jeer at us. For some time, I was afraid that someday I also might not be convinced of the futility of our own programme. That was a turning point in my revolutionary career. "Study" was the cry that reverberated in the corridors of my mind. Study to enable yourself with arguments in favour of your cult. I began to study. My previous faith and convictions underwent methods alone which was so prominent amongst our predecessors, was replaced by serious ideas. No more mysticism, no more blind faith. Realism became our cult. Use of force became justifiable when resorted to as a matter of terrible necessity: non-violence, as a policy, became indispensable for all mass movements. So much about methods. The most important thing was the clear conception of the ideal for which we were to fight. As there were no important activities in the field of action I got ample opportunity to study various ideals of the world revolution. I studied Bakunin, the anarchist leader, something of Marx, the father of communism, and much of Lenin, Trotsky and others—the men who had successfully carried out a revolution in their country. They were all atheists. Bakunin's *God and State*, though only fragmentary, is an interesting study of the subject. Later still, I came across a book entitled *Common Sense* by Soham Swami. It was only a sort of mystic atheism. This subject became of utmost interest to me. By the end of 1926, I had been convinced as to the baselessness of the theory of existence of an almighty supreme being who created, guided, and controlled the universe. I had given out this disbelief of mine. I began discussion on the subjects with my friends. I had become a pronounced atheist. But what it meant will presently be discussed.

In May 1927, I was arrested at Lahore. The arrest was a surprise. I was quite unaware of the fact that the police wanted me. All of a sudden, while passing through a garden, I found myself surrounded by police. To my own surprise, I was very calm at that time. I did not feel any sensation, nor did I experience any excitement. I was taken into police custody. Next day, I was taken to the Railway Police lock-up where I was to spend a whole month. After several conversations with the police officials for days on end, I guessed that they had some information regarding my connection with the Kakori party and my other activities in connection with the revolutionary movement. They told me that I had been to Lucknow while the trial was going on there, that I had negotiated a certain scheme about their rescue, that after obtaining their approval, we had procured some bombs, that by way of test, one of the bombs was thrown in the crowd on the occasion of Dussehra in 1926. They further informed me, in my interest, that if I could give any statement throwing some light on the activities of the revolutionary party, I was not to be imprisoned but on the contrary set free and rewarded, even without being produced as an approver in the court. I laughed at the proposal. It was all humbug. People holding ideas like ours do not throw bombs on their own innocent people. One fine morning Mr. Newman, the then Senior Superintendent of C.I.D., came to me. And after much sympathetic talk with me, imparted to me the extremely sad news that if I did not give any statement as demanded by them, they would be forced to send me up for trial for conspiracy to wage war in connection with Kakori Case and for brutal murders in connection with Dussehra bomb outrage. And he further informed me that they had evidence enough to get me convicted and hanged. In those days, I believed—though I was quite innocent—the police could do it if they desired. That very day certain police officials began to persuade me to offer my prayers to God regularly, both the times. Now I was an atheist. I wanted to settle for myself whether it was in the days of peace and enjoyment alone that I could boast of being an atheist or whether during such hard times as well; I could stick to those principles of mine. After great consideration, I decided that I could not lead myself to believe in and pray to God. No, I never did. That was the real test and I came out successful. Never for a moment did I desire to save my neck at the cost of certain other things. So, I was a staunch disbeliever; and have ever since been. It was not an easy job to stand that test. 'Belief' softens the hardships, even can make them pleasant. In God, man can find very strong consolation and support. Without Him, man has to depend upon himself. To stand upon one's own legs amid storms and hurricanes is not a child's play. At such testing moments, vanity—if any— evaporates and man cannot dare to defy the general beliefs. If he does, then we must conclude that he has got certain other strength than mere vanity. This is exactly the situation now. Judgment is already too well-known. Within a week it is to be pronounced. What is the consolation with the exception of the idea that I am going to sacrifice my life for a cause? A God-believing Hindu might be expecting to be reborn as a king, a Muslim or a Christian might dream of the luxuries to be enjoyed in paradise and the reward he is to get for his suffering and sacrifices. But, what am I to expect? I know the moment the rope is fitted around my neck and rafters removed under my feet, that will be the final moment—that will be the last moment. I, or to be more precise, my soul, as interpreted in the metaphysical terminology shall all be finished there. Nothing further. A short life of struggle with no such magnificent end, shall in itself be the reward, if I have the courage to take it in that light. That is all. With no selfish motive or desire to be awarded here or hereafter, quite disinterestedly, have I devoted my life to the cause of independence, because I could not do otherwise. The day we find a great number of men and women, who cannot devote themselves to anything else than the service of mankind and emancipation of the suffering humanity, that day shall inaugurate the era of liberty. Not to become a king, nor to gain any other rewards here, or in the next birth or after death in paradise, shall they be inspired to challenge the oppressors, exploiters, and tyrants, but to cast off the yoke of serfdom from the neck of humanity and to establish liberty and peace shall they tread this—to their individual selves perilous and to their noble selves the only glorious imaginable—path. Is the pride in their noble cause to be misinterpreted as vanity? Who dares to utter such an abominable epithet? To him, I say either he is a fool or a knave. Let us forgive him for he cannot realize the depth, the emotion, the sentiment and the noble feelings that surge in that heart. His heart is dead as a mere lump of flesh, his eyes are weak, the evils of other interests having been cast over them. Self-reliance is always liable to be interpreted as vanity. It is sad and miserable but there is no help.

You go and oppose the prevailing faith; you go and criticize a hero, a great man who is generally believed to be above criticism because he is thought to be infallible, the strength of your argument shall force the multitude to decry you as vainglorious. This is due to the mental stagnation. Criticism and independent thinking are the two indispensable qualities of a revolutionary. Because Mahatamaji is great, therefore, none should criticize him. Because he has risen above, therefore everything he says—may be in the field of politics or religion, economics or ethics— is right. Whether you are convinced or not, you must say: "Yes, that's true." This mentality does not lead towards progress. It is rather too obviously reactionary.

Because our forefathers had set up a faith in some supreme being—the Almighty God—therefore, any man who dares to challenge the validity of that faith, or the very existence of that Supreme Being, he shall have to be called an apostate, a renegade. If his argument are too sound to be refuted by counter-arguments and spirit too strong to be cowed down by the threat of misfortunes that may befall him by the wrath of the Almighty, he shall be decried as vainglorious, his spirit to be denominated as vanity. Then, why do waste time in this vain discussion? Why try to argue out the whole thing? This question is coming before the public for the first time, and is being handled in this matter of fact way for the first time, hence this lengthy discussion.

As for the first question, I think I have cleared that it is not vanity that has led me to atheism. My way of argument has proved to be convincing or not, that is to be judged by my readers, not me. I know in the present circumstances my faith in God would have made my life easier, my burden lighter, and my disbelief in Him has turned all the circumstances too dry, and the situation may assume too harsh a shape. A little bit of mysticism can make it poetical. But I do not want the help of any intoxication to meet my fate. I am a realist. I have been trying to overpower the instinct in me by the help of reason. I have not always been successful in achieving this end. But a man's duty is to try and endeavour, success depends upon chance and environments.

As for the second question that if it was not vanity, then there ought to be some reason to disbelieve the old and still prevailing faith of the existence of God. Yes, I come to that now. Reason there is. According to me, any man who has got some reasoning power at his command always tries to reason out his environments. Where direct proofs are lacking, philosophy occupies the important place. As I have already stated, a certain revolutionary friend used to say that philosophy is the outcome of human weakness. When our ancestors had leisure enough to try to solve out the mystery of this world, its past, present, and the future, its whys and wherefores, they having been terribly short of direct proofs, everybody tried to solve the problem in his own way. Hence, we find the wide differences in the fundamentals of various religious creeds, which sometimes assume very antagonistic and conflicting shapes. Not only the Oriental and Occidental philosophies differ, there are differences even amongst various schools of thought in each hemisphere. Amongst Oriental religions, the Moslem faith is not at all compatible with Hindu faith. In India alone, Buddhism and Jainism are sometimes quite separate from Brahmanism, in which there are again conflicting faiths as Arya Samaj and Sanatan Dharma. Charwak is still another independent thinker of the past ages. He challenged the authority of God in the old times. All these creeds differ from each other on the fundamental question; and everybody considers himself to be on the right. There lies the misfortune. Instead of using the experiments and expressions of the ancient Savants and thinkers as a basis for our future struggle against ignorance and to try to find out a solution to this mysterious problem, we, lethargical as we have proved to be, raise the hue and cry of faith, unflinching and unwavering faith to their versions and thus are guilty of stagnation in human progress.

Any man who stands for progress has to criticize, disbelieve, and challenge every item of the old faith. Item by item he has to reason out every nook and corner of the prevailing faith. If, after considerable reasoning, one is led to believe in any theory or philosophy, his faith is welcomed. His reasoning can be mistaken, wrong, misled, and sometimes fallacious. But he is liable to correction because reason is the guiding star of his life. But mere faith and blind faith is dangerous: it dulls the brain and makes a man reactionary. A man, who claims to be a realist, has to challenge the whole of the ancient faith. If it does not stand the onslaught of reason, it crumbles down. Then, the first thing for him is to shatter the whole down and clear a space for the erection of a new philosophy. This is the negative side. Thereafter, it begins the positive work in which sometimes some material of he old faith may be used for the purpose of reconstruction. As far as I am concerned, let me admit at the very outset that I have not been able to study much on this point. I had a great desire to study the Oriental philosophy but I could not get any chance or opportunity to do the same. But so far as the negative study is under discussion, I think I am convinced to the extent of questioning the soundness of the old faith. I have been convinced as to non-existence of a conscious supreme being who is guiding and directing the movements of nature. We believe in nature and the whole progressive movement aims at the domination of man over nature for his service. There is no conscious power behind it to direct. This is what our philosophy is.

As for the negative side, we ask a few questions from the 'believers'.

(1) If, as you believe, there is an almighty, omnipresent, omniscient, and omnipotent God, who created the earth or world, please let me know why did he create it? This world of woes and miseries, a veritable, eternal combination of numberless tragedies! Not a single soul being perfectly satisfied.

Pray, don't say that it is His law! If he is bound by any law, he is not omnipotent. He is another slave like ourselves. Please don't say that it is his enjoyment. Nero burnt one Rome. He killed a very limited number of people. He created very few tragedies, all to his perfect enjoyment. And, what is his place in history? By what names do the historians mention him? All the venomous epithets are showered upon him. Pages are blackened with invective diatribes condemning Nero, the tyrant, the heartless, the wicked. One Changezkhan sacrificed a few thousand lives to seek pleasure in it and we hate the very name. Then, how are you going to justify your almighty, eternal Nero, who has been, and is still causing numberless tragedies every day, every hour, and every minute? How do you think to support his misdoings which surpass those of Changez every single moment? I say why did he create this world—a veritable hell, a place of constant and bitter unrest? Why did the Almighty create man when he had the power not to do it? What is the justification for all this? Do you say, to award the innocent sufferers hereafter and to punish the wrongdoers as well? Well, well: How far shall you justify a man who may dare to inflict wounds upon your body to apply a very soft and soothing ointment upon it afterwards? How far the supporters and organizers of the Gladiator institution were justified in throwing men before the half-starved furious lions to be cared for and well-locked after if they could survive and manage to escape death by the wild beasts? That is why I ask: Why did the conscious Supreme Being create this world and man in it? To seek pleasure? Where, then, is the difference between him and Nero?

You Mohammadens and Christians! Hindu philosophy shall still linger on to offer another argument. I ask you, what is your answer to the above-mentioned question? You don't believe in previous birth. Like Hindus, you cannot advance the argument of previous misdoings of the apparently quite innocent suffers. I ask you, why did the omnipotent labour for six days to create the world though word and each day to say that all was well? Call him today. Show him the past history. Make him study the present situation. Let us see if he dares to say: "All is well."

From the dungeons of prisons, from the stores of starvation consuming millions upon millions of human beings in slums and huts, from the exploited labourers, patiently or say apathetically watching the procedure of their blood being sucked by the Capitalist vampires, and the wastage of human energy that will make a man with the least common sense shiver with horror, and from the preference of throwing the surplus of production in oceans rather than to distribute amongst the needy producers—to the palaces of kings built upon the foundation laid with human bones... let him see all this and let him say: "All is well." Why and wherefore? That is my question. You are silent. Alright then, I proceed.

Well, you Hindus, you say all the present sufferers belong to the class of sinners of the previous births. Good. You say the present oppressors were saintly people in their previous births, hence, they enjoy power. Let me admit that your ancestors were very shrewd people; they tried to find out theories strong enough to hammer down all the efforts of reason and disbelief. But let us analyze how this argument can really stand.

From the point of view of the most famous jurists, punishment can be justified only from three or four ends, to meet which it is inflicted upon the wrongdoer. They are retributive, reformative, and deterrent. The retributive theory is now being condemned by all the advanced thinkers. Deterrent theory is also following the same fate. Reformative theory is the only one which is essential and indispensable for human progress. It aims at returning the offender as a most competent and a peace-loving citizen to the society. But, what is the nature of punishment inflicted by God upon men, even if we suppose them to be offenders? You say he sends them to be born as a cow, a cat, a tree, a herb, or a beast. You enumerate these punishments to be 84 lakhs. I ask you: what is its reformative effect upon man? How many men have you met who say that they were born as a donkey in previous birth for having committed any sin? None. Don't quote your Puranas. I have no scope to touch your mythologies. Moreover, do you know that the greatest sin in this world is to be poor? Poverty is a sin, it is a punishment. I ask you how far would you appreciate a criminologist, a jurist, or a legislator who proposes such measures of punishment which shall inevitably force men to commit more offences. Had not your God thought of this, or he also had to learn these things by experience, but at the cost of untold sufferings to be borne by humanity? What do you think shall be the fate of a man who has been born in a poor and illiterate family of, say, a chamar or a sweeper? He is poor hence he cannot study. He is hated and shunned by his fellow human beings who think themselves to be his superiors having been born in, say, a higher caste. His ignorance, his poverty, and the treatment meted out to him shall harden his heart towards society. Suppose he commits a sin, who shall bear the consequences? God, he himself, or the learned ones of the society? What about the punishment of those people who were deliberately kept ignorant by the haughty and egotist Brahmans, and who had to pay the penalty by bearing the stream of being led(lead) in their ears for having heard a few sentences of your sacred books of learning—the Vedas? If they committed any offence—who was to be responsible for them and who was to bear the brunt? My dear friends! These theories are the inventions of the privileged ones! They justify their usurped power, riches and superiority by the help of these theories. Yes! It was perhaps Upton Sinclair that wrote at some place that just makes a man a believer in immortality and then rob him of all his riches and possessions. He shall help you even in that ungrudgingly. The coalition among the religious preachers and possessors of power brought forth jails, gallows, knouts and these theories.

I ask why your omnipotent God does not stop every man when he is committing any sin or offence? He can do it quite easily. Why did he not kill warlords or kill the fury of war in them and thus avoid the catastrophe hurled down on the head of humanity by the Great War? Why does he not just produce a certain sentiment in the mind of the British people to liberate India? Why does he not infuse the altruistic enthusiasm in the hearts of all capitalists to forego their rights of personal possessions of means of production and thus redeem the whole labouring community—nay, the whole human society, from the bondage of capitalism? You want to reason out the practicability of socialist theory; I leave it for your almighty to enforce it. People recognize the merits of socialism in as much as the general welfare is concerned. They oppose it under the pretext of its being impracticable. Let the Almighty step in and arrange everything in an orderly fashion. Now don't try to advance round about arguments, they are out of order. Let me tell you, British rule is here not because God wills it, but because they possess power and we do not dare to oppose them. Not that it is with the help of God that they are keeping us under their subjection, but it is with the help of guns and rifles, bomb and bullets, police and militia, and our apathy, that they are successfully committing the most deplorable sin against society—the outrageous exploitation of one nation by another. Where is God? What is he doing? Is he enjoying all these woes of human race? A Nero; a Changez!! Down with him!

Do you ask me how I explain the origin of this world and origin of man? Alright, I tell you, Charles Darwin has tried to throw some light on the subject. Study him. Read Soham Swami's *Common Sense*. It shall answer your question to some extent. This is a phenomenon of nature. The accidental mixture of different substances in the shape of nebulae produced this earth. When? Consult history. The same process produced animals and, in the long run, man. Read Darwin's *On The Origin of Species*. And all the later progress is due to man's constant conflict with nature and his efforts to override it. This is the briefest possible explanation of the phenomenon.

Your other argument may be just to ask why a child is born blind or lame if not due to his deeds committed in the previous birth? This problem has been explained away by biologists as a mere biological phenomenon. According to them, the whole burden rests upon the shoulders of the parents who may be conscious or ignorant of their own deeds which led to mutilation of the child previous to its birth.

Naturally, you may ask another question—though it is quite childish in essence. If no God existed, how did the people come to believe in him? My answer is clear and brief. As they came to believe in ghosts and evil spirits; the only difference is that belief in God is almost universal and the philosophy well-developed. Unlike certain radicals, I would not attribute its origin to the ingenuity of the exploiters who wanted to keep the people under their subjection by preaching the existence of a supreme being and then claiming an authority and sanction from him for their privileged positions, though I do not differ with them on the essential point that all faiths, religions, creeds, and such other institutions became in turn the mere supporters of the tyrannical and exploiting institutions, men and classes. Rebellion against king is always a sin, according to every religion.

As regards the origin of God, my own idea is that having realized the limitation of man, his weaknesses and shortcomings having been taken into consideration, God was brought into imaginary existence to encourage man to face boldly all the trying circumstances, to meet all dangers manfully and to check and restrain his outbursts in prosperity and affluence. God, both his private laws and parental generosity, was imagined and painted in greater details. He was to serve as a deterrent factor when his fury and private laws were discussed, so that man may not become a danger to society. He was to serve as a father, mother, sister and brother, friend and helper, when his parental qualifications were to be explained. So that when man be in great distress, having been betrayed and deserted by all friends, he may find consolation in the idea that an ever-true friend, was still there to help him, to support him and that he was almighty and could do anything. Really that was useful to the society in the primitive age. The idea of God is helpful to man in distress.

Society has to fight out this belief as well as the idol worship and the narrow conception of religion. Similarly, when man tries to stand on his own legs and becomes a realist, he shall have to throw the faith aside, and face manfully all the distress, trouble, in which the circumstances may throw him. That is exactly my state of affairs. It is not my vanity, my friends. It is my mode of thinking that has made me an atheist. I don't know whether, in my case, belief in God and offering of daily prayers which I consider to be most selfish and degraded act on the part of man, whether these prayers can prove to be helpful or they shall make my case worse still. I have read of atheists facing all troubles quite boldly; so am I trying to stand like a man with an erect head to the last; even on the gallows.

Let us see how I carry on. One friend asked me to pray. When informed of my atheism, he said, "During your last days you will begin to believe!" I said, "No, dear sir, it shall not be. I will think that to be an act of degradation and demoralization on my part. For selfish motives I am not going to pray." Readers and friends, "Is this vanity?", if it is, I stand for it.

18

"Show the World That the Revolutionaries Not Only Die for Their Ideals but Can Face Every Calamity!"
Bhagat Singh Wrote to B. K. Dutt (November, 1930)

This letter gives an idea as to what Bhagat Singh expected from those comrades who would escape capital punishment.

Central Jail,
November, 1930

Dear Brother,

The judgment has been delivered. I am condemned to death. In these cells, besides myself, there are many others prisoners who are waiting to be hanged. The only prayer of these people is that somehow or the other they may escape the noose. Perhaps, I am the only man amongst them who is anxiously waiting for the day when I will be fortunate enough to embrace the gallows for my ideal.

I will climb the gallows gladly and show the world as to how bravely the revolutionaries can sacrifice themselves for the cause.

I will have condemned to death, but you are sentenced to transportation for life. You will live and, while living, you will have to show to the world that the revolutionaries not only die for their ideals but can face every calamity. Death should not be a means to escape the worldly difficulties.

Those revolutionaries who have by chance escaped the gallows for the ideal but also bear the worst type of tortures in the dark, dingy prison cells.

Yours,
Bhagat Singh

19

"I Want to Tell You That Obstacles Make a Man Perfect"
Bhagat Singh Wrote to Sukhdev on Suicide
(1930)

The hearing of the case was over. Judgment was expected any day. Sukhdev expected life transportation for him. To him, the idea of being confined in jail for 20 years was repulsive. He wrote to Bhagat Singh that in case he (Sukhdev) is convicted for life, he will commit suicide. He stood for release or death; no middle course.

Bhagat Singh's reaction to Sukhdev's letter was very sharp. Serve, suffer, and live to struggle for the cause—that was his stand. "Escaping from hardships is cowardice," he said. This letter provides one more window to peep into the martyr's mind.

Dear Brother,

I have gone through your letter attentively and many times. I realize that the changed situation has affected us differently. The things you hated outside have now become essential to you. In the same way, the things I used to support strongly are of no significance to me anymore. For example, I believed in personal love, but now this feeling has ceased to occupy any particular position in my heart and mind. While outside, you were strongly opposed to it but now a drastic change and radicalization is apparent in your ideas about it. You experience it as an extremely essential part of human existence and you have found a particular kind of happiness in the experience.

You may still recollect that one day I had discussed suicide with you. That time I told you that in some situations suicide may be justifiable, but you contested my point. I vividly remember the time and place of our conversation. We talked about this in the Shahanshahi Kutia one evening. You said in jest that such a cowardly act can never be justified. You said that acts of this kind were horrible and heinous, but I see that you have now made an about-turn on this subject. Now, you find it not only proper in certain situations but also necessary, even essential. My opinion is what you had held earlier, that suicide is a heinous crime. It is an act of complete cowardice. Leave alone revolutionaries, no individual can ever justify such an act.

You say you fail to understand how suffering alone can serve the country. Such a question from a person like you is really perplexing, because how much thoughtfully we loved the motto of the Naujawan Bharat Sabha—"to suffer and sacrifice through service". I believe that you served as much as it was possible. Now is the time when you should suffer for what you did. Another point is that this is exactly the moment when you have to lead the entire people.

Man acts only when he is sure of the justness of his action, as we threw the bomb in the Legislative Assembly. After the action, it is the time for bearing the consequences of that act. Do you think that had we tried to avoid the punishment by pleading for mercy, we would have been more justified? No, this would have had an adverse effect on the masses. We are now quite successful in our endeavour.

At the time of our imprisonment, the conditions for the political prisoners of our party were very miserable. We tried to improve that. I tell you quite seriously that we believed we would die soon. Neither we were aware of the technique of forced feeding nor did we ever think of it. We were ready to die. Do you mean to say that we were intending to commit suicide? No. Striving and sacrificing one's life for a superior ideal can never be called suicide. We are envious of the death of our Comrade Yatindra Nath Das. Will you call it suicide? Ultimately, our sufferings bore fruit. A big movement started in the whole of the country. We were successful in our aim. Death in the struggles of this kind is an ideal death.

Apart from this, the comrades among us, who believe that they will be awarded death, should await that day patiently when the sentence will be announced and they will be hanged. This death will also be beautiful, but committing suicide—to cut short the life just to avoid some pain—is cowardice. I want to tell you that obstacles make a man perfect. Neither you nor I, rather none of us, have suffered any pain so far. That part of our life has started only now.

You will recollect that we have talked several times about realism in the Russian literature, which is nowhere visible in our own. We highly appreciate the situations of pain in their stories, but we do not feel that spirit of suffering within ourselves. We also admire their passion and the extraordinary height of their characters, but we never bother to find out the reason. I will say that only the reference to their resolve to bear pain has produced the intensity, the suffering of pain, and this has given great depth and height to their characters and literature. We become pitiable and ridiculous when we imbibe an unreasoned mysticism in our life without any natural or substantial basis. People like us, who are proud to be a revolutionary in every sense, should always be prepared to bear all the difficulties, anxieties, pain and suffering which we invite upon ourselves by the struggles initiated by us and for which we call ourselves revolutionary.

I want to tell you that in jail, and in jail alone, can a person get an occasion to study empirically the great social subjects of crime and sin. I have read some literature on this and only the jail is the proper place for the self-study on all these topics. The best parts of the self-study for one is to suffer oneself.

You know it that the suffering of political prisoners in the jails of Russia caused, in the main, the revolution in the prison administration after the overthrow of Czardom. Is India not in need of such persons who are fully aware of this problem and have personal experience of these things? It will not suffice to say that someone else would do it, or that many other people are there to do it. Thus, men who find it quite dishonourable and hateful to leave the revolutionary responsibilities to others should start their struggle against the existing system with total devotion. They should violate these rules but they should also keep in mind the propriety, because unnecessary and improper attempts can never be considered just. Such agitations will shorten the process of revolution. All the arguments which you gave to keep yourself aloof from all such movement, are incomprehensible to me. Some of our friends are either fools or ignorant. They find your behaviour quite strange and incomprehensible. (They themselves say that they cannot comprehend it because you are above and very far from their understanding.)

In fact, if you feel that jail life is really humiliating, why don't you try to improve it by agitating? Perhaps, you will say that this struggle would be futile, but this is precisely the argument which is usually used as a cover by weak people to avoid participation in every movement. This is the reply which we kept on hearing outside the jail from the people who were anxious to escape from getting entangled in revolutionary movements. Shall I now hear the same argument from you? What could our party of a handful of people do in comparison to the vastness of its aims and ideals? Shall we infer from this that we erred gravely in starting our work altogether? No, inferences of this kind will be improper. This only shows the inner weakness of the man who thinks like this.

You write further that it cannot be expected of a man that he will have the same thinking after going through 14 long years of suffering in the prison, which he had before, because the jail life will crush all his ideas. May I ask you whether the situation outside the jail was any bit more favourable to our ideas? Even then, could we have left it because of our failures? Do you mean to imply that had we not entered the field, no revolutionary work would have taken place at all? If this be your contention, then you are mistaken, though it is right that we also proved helpful to an extent in changing the environment. But, the, we are only a product of the need of our times.

I shall even say that Marx—the father of communism—did not actually originate this idea. The Industrial Revolution of Europe itself produced men of this kind. Marx was one among them. Of course, Marx was also instrumental to an extent in gearing up the wheels of his time in a particular way.

I (and you, too) did not give birth to the ideas of socialism and communism in this country; this is the consequence of the effects of our time and situations upon ourselves. Of course, we did a bit to propagate these ideas, and, therefore, I say that since we have already taken a tough task upon ourselves, we should continue to advance it. The people will not be guided by our committing suicides to escape the difficulties; on the contrary, this will be quite a reactionary step.

We continued our work despite the testing environment of disappointments, pressures and violence ordained by the jail rules. While we worked, we were made target of many kinds of difficulties. Even men who were proud to proclaim themselves to be great revolutionaries, deserted us. Were these conditions not testing in the extreme? Then, what was the reason and the logic of continuing our agitation and efforts?

Does this simple argument not by itself give added strength to our ideas? And, don't we have instances of our revolutionary comrades who suffered for their convictions in jails and are still working on return from jails? Had Bakunin argued like you, he would have committed suicide right in the beginning. Today, you find many revolutionaries occupying responsible posts in the Russian state who had passed the greater part of their lives in prison, completing their sentences. Man must try hard to stick to his beliefs. No one can say what future has in store.

Do you remember that when we were discussing that some concentrated and effective poison should also be kept in our bomb factories, you opposed it very vehemently? The very idea was repugnant to you. You had no faith in it. So, what has happened now? Here, even the difficult and complex conditions do not obtain. I feel revulsion even in discussing this question. You hated even that attitude of mind which permits suicide. You will kindly excuse me for saying that had you acted according to this belief right at the time of your imprisonment (that is, you had committed suicide by taking poison), you would have served the revolutionary cause, but at this moment, even the thought of such an act is harmful to our cause.

There is just one more point which I will like to draw your attention to. We do not believe in God, hell and heaven, punishment and rewards, that is in any Godly accounting of human life. Therefore, we must think of life and death on materialist lines. When I was brought here from Delhi for the purpose of identification, some intelligence officers talked to me on this topic, in the presence of my father. They said that since I did not try to save of my life by divulging secrets, it proved the presence of an acute agony in my life. They argued that a death of this kind will be something like suicide. But I had replied that a man with beliefs and ideal like mine, could never think of dying uselessly. We want to get the maximum value for our lives. We want to serve humanity as much as possible. Particularly a man like me, whose life is nowhere sad or worried, can never think of suicide even, leave alone attempting it. The same thing I want to tell you now.

I hope you will permit me to tell you what I think about myself. I am certain of capital punishment for me. I do not expect even a bit of moderation or amnesty. Even if there is amnesty, it will not be for all, and even that amnesty will be for other only, not for us; it will be extremely restricted and burdened with various conditions. For us, neither there can be any amnesty nor it will ever happen. Even then, I wish that release calls for us should be made collectively and globally. Along with that, I also wish that when the movement reaches its climax, we should be hanged. It is my wish that if at any time any honourable and fair compromise is possible, issue like our case may never obstruct it. When the fate of the country is being decided, the fate of individuals should be forgotten. As revolutionaries, we do not believe that there can be any sudden change in the attitude of our rulers, particularly in the British race. Such a surprising change is impossible without sustained striving, sufferings and sacrifices. And it shall be achieved. As far as my attitude is concerned, I can welcome facilities and amnesty for all only when its effect is permanent and some indelible impressions are made on the hearts of the people of the country through our hanging. Only this much and nothing more.

20

Hunger-Strikers' Demands Reiterated
(January, 1930)

The Lahore Conspiracy Case (LCC) prisoners had suspended their hunger strike on the assurance that the Government of India was considering the Jail Committee Report and that the jail reformers would be punished for participating in the hunger strike. After the hunger strike was suspended, the GOI, however, resorted to delaying tactics. Disciplinary action was also taken against hunger strikers in U.P. and Punjab jails (other than LCC prisoners). It was in this connection that Bhagat Singh wrote this letter to the GOI, which was short of a notice-cum-ultimatum for resuming the hunger strike.

The Home Member,
The Govt. of India
Delhi

Through

The Special Magistrate,
Lahore Conspiracy Case,
Lahore

Sir,

With reference to our telegram dated January 20, 1930, reading as follows, we have not been given any reply.

Home Member Government. Delhi Under trials, Lahore Conspiracy Case and other Political Prisoners suspended hunger-strike on the assurance that the Indian Govt. was considering Provincial Jail Committee's reports. All Government Conference over. No action yet taken. As vindictive treatment to political prisoners still continues, we request we be informed within a week final Government decision. Lahore Conspiracy Case under trials.

As briefly stated in the above telegram, we beg to bring to your kind notice that the Lahore Conspiracy Case under trials and several other political prisoners confined in Punjab jails suspended hunger strike on the assurance given by the members of the Punjab Jail Enquiry Committee that the question of the treatment of political prisoners was going to be finally settled to our satisfaction within a very short period. Further, after the death of our great martyr Jatindra Nath Das, the matter was taken up in the Legislative Assembly and the same assurance was given publicly by Sir James Crerar. It was then pronounced that there has been a change of heart and the question of the treatment of political prisoners was receiving the utmost sympathy of the government. Such political prisoners who were still on hunger strike in jails of the different parts of the country then suspended their hunger strike on the request being made to this effect in an AICC resolution passed in view of the said assurance and the critical condition of some of the prisoners.

Since then all the local governments have submitted their reports. A meeting of Inspectors-General of Prisons of different provinces has been held at Lucknow and the deliberations of the All-India Government Conference have been concluded at Delhi. The All-India Conference was held in the month of December last, but not carried into effect any final recommendations. By such dilatory attitude of the government we no less than the general public have begun to fear that perhaps the question has been shelved. Our apprehensions have been strengthened by the vindictive treatment meted out to hunger strikers and other political prisoners during the last four months. It is very difficult for us to know the details of the hardships to which the political prisoners are being subjected. Still the little information that has trickled out of the four walls of the jails in sufficient to furnish us with glaring instances. We give below a few such instances which we cannot but feel, are not in conformity with the government assurance.

1. Sj. B.K. Banerji, undergoing five years' imprisonment in connection with Dakshineshwar Bomb Case in Lahore Central Jail, joined the hunger strike last year. Now as a punishment for the same, for each day of his period of hunger strike, two days of the remission so far earned by him have been forfeited. Under usual circumstances his release was due in December last, but it will be delayed by full four months. In the same jail, similar punishment has been awarded to Baba Sohan Singh, an old man of about 70, now undergoing his sentence of life transportation in connection with the (first) Lahore Conspiracy Case. Besides, among others, Sardar Gopal Singh confined in Mianwali Jail, Master Mota Singh confined in Rawalpindi Jail have also been awarded vindictive punishments for joining the general hunger strike. In most of these cases the periods of imprisonment have been enhanced while some of them have been removed from the Special class.

2. For the same offence, i.e., joining the general hunger strike, Messrs Sachindra Nath Sanyal, Ram Kishan Khattri, and Suresh Chandra Bhattacharya, confined in Agra Central Jail, Raj Kumar Sinha, Sachindra Nath Bukshi, Manmath Nath Gupta, and several other Kakori

case prisoners have been severely punished. It is reliably learnt that Mr. Sanyal was given bar-fetters and solitary confinement and as a consequence there has been a break down in his health. His weight has gone down by 18 pounds. Mr. Bhattacharya is reported to be suffering from tuberculosis. The three Bareilly Jail prisoners also have been punished. It is learnt that all their privileges have been withdrawn. Even their usual rights of interviewing with relations and communication with them were forfeited. They have all been considerably reduced in their weights. Two press statements have been issued in this connection in September 1929 and January 1930 by Pandit Jawaharlal Nehru.

3. After the passing of the AICC resolution regarding hunger strike, the copies of the same, which were sent to different political prisoners, were withheld by the jail authorities. Further, the govt. refused a Congress deputation to meet the prisoners in this respect.

4. The Lahore Conspiracy Case under trials were assaulted brutally on October 23 and 24, 1929, by orders of high police officials. Full details have appeared in the press. The copy of the statement of the one of us recorded by the Special Magistrate, Pt. Shri Krishan, has been duly forwarded to you in a communication dated December 16, 1929 Neither the Punjab Government nor the Govt. of India felt it necessary to reply or even acknowledge receipt of our communication praying for an enquiry. While, on the other hand, local government has felt the imperative necessity of prosecuting us in connection with the very same incident for offering "violent resistance".

5. In the last week of December 1929, Sj. Kiran Chandra Das and eight others confined in the Lahore Borstal Jail, when being taken to and produced in the Magistrate's Court, were found handcuffed and chained together in flagrant breach of the unanimous recommendations of the Punjab Jail Enquiry Committee and also of Inspector-General of Prisons, Punjab. It is further noteworthy that these prisoners were under trials, changed for a bailable offence. A long statement issued by Dr. Mohd. Aslam, Lala Duni Chand of Lahore, and Lala Duni Chand of Ambala in this connection was published in *Tribune*.

When we learnt these and other sufferings of the political prisoners we refrained from resuming our hunger strike, though we were much grieved as we thought that the matter was going to be finally settled at an early date, but in the light of the above instances, are we now to believe that the untold sufferings of the hunger strikers and the supreme sacrifice made by Jatin Das have all been in vain? Are we to understand that the government gave its assurance only to check the growing tide of public agitation and to avert a crisis? You will agree with us if we say that we have waited patiently for a sufficiently reasonable period of time. But we cannot wait indefinitely. The government, by its dilatory attitude and the continuation of vindictive treatment to political prisoners, has left us no other option but to resume the struggle. We realize that to go on hunger strike and to carry it on is no easy task. But let us at the same time point out that India can produce many more Jatins and Wagias, Ran Rakshas and Bhan Singhs. (The last two laid down their lives in the Andamans in 1917—the first breathed his last after

63 days of hunger strike, while the other died the death of a great hero after silently undergoing in human tortures for full six months.)

Enough has been said by us and the members of the public (inquiry committee) in justification of the better treatment of political prisoners and it is unnecessary here to repeat the same. We would however like to say a few words as regards the inclusion of motive as the basis and the most important factor in the matter of classification. Great fuss has been created on the question of criteria of classification. We find that motive has altogether been excluded so far from the criteria suggested by different provincial governments. This is a really strange attitude. It is through motive alone that the real value of any action can be decided. Are we to understand that the government is unable to distinguish between a robber who robs and kills his victim and a Kharag Bahadur who kills a villain and saves the honour of a young lady and redeems society of a most licentious parasite? Are both to be treated as two men belonging to the same category? Is there no difference between two men who commit the same offence, one guided buy selfish motive and the other by a selfless one? Similarly, is there no difference between a common murderer and a political worker, even if the latter resorts to violence? Does not his selflessness elevate his place from amongst those of ordinary criminals? In these circumstances, we think that motive should be held as the most important factor in the criteria for classification.

Last year, in the beginning of our hunger strike, when public leaders, including Dr. Gopi Chand and Lala Duni Chand of Ambala—the last named being one of the signatories to the Punjab Jail Enquiry Committee Report —approached us to discuss the same thing and when they told us that the government considered to treat the political prisoners convicted of offences of violent nature as Special class prisoners, then, by way of compromise, we agreed to the proposal to the extent of excluding those actually charged with murder. However, later on, the discussion took a different turn and the communiqué containing the terms of reference for the Punjab Jail Enquiry Committee was so worded that the question of motive seemed to be altogether excluded, and the classification was based on two thing:

1. Nature of offence; and

2. Social status of "offender".

These criteria, instead of solving the problem, made it all the more complicated.

We could understand two classes amongst the political prisoners, those charged for non-violent offences and those charged for violent offences. But then creeps in the question of social status in the report of the Punjab Jail Enquiry Committee. As Chaudhary Afzal Haque has pointed out, and rightly too, in his note of dissent to this report, what will be the fate of those political workers who have been reduced to pauper's conditions due to their honorary services in the cause of freedom? Are they to be left at the mercy of a magistrate who will away try to prove the bonafide of his loyalty by classifying everyone as an ordinary convict? Or, is it expected that a non-cooperator will stretch his hand before the people against whom he is fighting as an opponent, begging for better treatment in jail? Is this the way of removing the causes of dissatisfaction, or rather intensifying them? It might be argued that people living in poverty outside the jails, should not expect luxuries inside the prison when they are detained for the purpose of punishment. But, are the reforms that are demanded, of a nature of luxury? Are they not the bare necessities of life, according to the most moderate standard of living? Inspite of all the facilities that can possibly be demanded, jail will ever remain a jail. The prison, in itself, does not contain and can never contain any magnetic power to attract the people from outside. Nobody will commit offences simply to come to jail. Moreover, may we venture to say that it is a very poor argument on the part of any government to say that its citizens have been driven to such extreme destitution that their standard of living has fallen even lower than that of jails? Does not such an argument cut at the very root of that government's right of existence? Anyhow, we are not concerned with that, at present. What we want to say is that the best way to remove the prevailing dissatisfaction would be to classify the political prisoners as such into a separate class which may further be subdivided, if need be, into two classes—one for those convicted of non-violent offences and the other for persons whose offences include violence. In that case, motive will become one of the deciding factors. To say that motive cannot be ascertained in political cases is hypocritical assertion. What is it that today informs the jail authorities to deprive the 'political' even of the ordinary privileges? What it is that deprives them of the special grades or 'nambardaries', etc.? What does make the authorities to keep them aloof and separated from all other convicts? The same thing can help in the classification as well.

As for the special demands, we have already stated them in full in our memorandum to the Punjab Jail Enquiry Committee. We would, however, particularly emphasize that no political prisoner, whatever his offence may be, should be given any hard and undignified labour for which he may not feel aptitude. All of them, confined in one jail, should be kept together in the same ward. At least one standard daily newspaper in vernacular or English should be given to them. Full and proper facilities for study should be granted. Lastly, they should be allowed to supplement their expenses for diet and clothing from their private sources.

We still hope that the government will carry into effect without further delay its promise made to us and to the public, so that there may not be another occasion for resuming the hunger strike. Unless and until we find a definite move on the part of the government to redeem its promise in the course of the next seven days, we shall be forced to resume the hunger strike.

Yours, etc.
Bhagat Singh, Dutt
others
Dated: January 28, 1930
Under trials, Lahore Conspiracy Case

21

"I Feel as Though I Have Been Stabbed in the Back"
Bhagat Singh Wrote to His Father from Jail
(October, 1930)

When the Lahore Conspiracy Case was in its final stage, Sardar Kishan Singh (Bhagat Singh's father) filed a petition with the Special Tribunal Lahore in September 1930 saying that there were many facts to prove that his son was innocent and that he had nothing to do with the junior British officer J.P. Sounder's murder. He also requested that his son be given an opportunity to prove his innocence. When Bhagat Singh, then a 23-year-old revolutionary, came to know of this, he raised objection and wrote a strongly-worded letter to his father protesting this move on October 4th. The letter was published days prior to the judgement of the case.

October 4, 1930

My Dear Father,

I was astounded to learn that you had submitted a petition to the members of the Special Tribunal in connection with my defence. This intelligence proved to be too severe a blow to be borne with equanimity. It has upset the whole equilibrium of my mind. I have not been able to understand how you could think it proper to submit such a petition at this stage and in these circumstances. In spite of all the sentiments and feelings of a father, I don't think you were at all entitled to make such a move on my behalf without even consulting me. You know that in the political field my views have always differed with those of yours. I have always been acting independently without having cared for your approval or disapproval.

I hope you can recall to yourself that since the very beginning you have been trying to convince me to fight my case very seriously and to defend myself properly. But you also know that I was always opposed to it. I never had any desire to defend myself and never did I seriously think about it. Whether it was a mere vague ideology or that I had certain arguments to justify my position, is a different question and that cannot be discussed here.

You know that we have been pursuing a definite policy in this trial. Every action of mine ought to have been consistent with that policy, my principle, and my programme. At present, the circumstances are altogether different, but had the situation been otherwise, even then I would have been the last man to offer defence. I had only one idea before me throughout the trial, i.e., to show complete indifference towards the trial in spite of serious nature of the charges against us. I have always been of opinion that all the political workers should be indifferent and should never bother about the legal fight in the law courts and should boldly bear the heaviest possible sentences inflicted upon them. They may defend themselves, but always from purely political considerations and never from a personal point of view. Our policy in this trial has always been consistent with this principle; whether we were successful in that or not is not for me to judge. We have always been doing our duty quite disinterestedly.

In the statement accompanying the text of Lahore Conspiracy Case Ordinance, the Viceroy had stated that the accused in this case were trying to bring both law and justice into contempt. The situation afforded us an opportunity to show the public whether we were trying to bring law into contempt or whether others were doing so. People might disagree with us on this point. You might be one of them. But that never meant that such moves should be made on my behalf without my consent or even my knowledge. My life is not so precious, at least to me, as you may probably think it to be. It is not at all worth buying at the cost of my principles. There are other comrades of mine whose cases are as serious as that of mine. We had adopted a common policy and we shall stand to the last, no matter how dearly we have to pay individually for it.

Father, I am quite perplexed. I fear I might overlook the ordinary principle of etiquette and my language may become a little harsh while criticizing or rather censoring this move on your part. Let me be candid. I feel as though I have been stabbed in the back. Had any other person done it, I would have considered it to be nothing short of treachery. But in your case, let me say that it has been a weakness—a weakness of the worst type.

This was the time where everybody's mettle was being tested. Let me say, father, you have failed. I know you are as sincere a patriot as one can be. I know you have devoted your life to the cause of Indian independence, but why, at this moment, have you displayed such a weakness? I cannot understand.

In the end, I would like to inform you and my other friends and all the people interested in my case, that I have not approved of your move. I am still not at all in favour of offering any defence. Even if the court had accepted that petition submitted by some of my co-accused regarding defence, etc., I would have not defended myself. My applications submitted to the Tribunal regarding my interview during the hunger strike, were misinterpreted and it was published in the press that I was going to offer defence, though in reality I was never willing to offer any defence. I still hold the same opinion as before. My friends in the Borstal Jail will be taking it as a treachery and betrayal on my part. I shall not even get an opportunity to clear my position before them.

I want that public should know all the details about this complication, and, therefore, I request you to publish this letter.

Your loving son,
Bhagat Singh

22

To Young Political Workers
(February, 1931)

Written on February 2, 1931, this document is a sort of behest to young political workers of India. At that time, the talk of some sort of compromise between the Congress and the British Government was in the air. Through this document, Bhagat Singh explained as to when a compromise is permissible and when it is not.

After Bhagat Singh's execution, this document was published in a mutilated form. All references to Soviet Union, Marx, Lenin, and the Communist Party were carefully deleted. Subsequently, the GOI published it in one of its secret reports in 1936. A photostat copy of the full report is preserved in the library of the Martyrs' Memorial and Freedom Struggle Research Centre at Lucknow.

[Mr. Shiv Verma ji, a compatriot and one of the closest comrades of Bhagat Singh in HSRA, was also a co-accused in Lahore Conspiracy Case. He wrote an introduction to this document which was written on February 2, 1931. This document is a sort of behest to young political workers of India. At that time, the talk of some sort of compromise between the Congress and the British Government was in the air. Through this document, Bhagat Singh explained as to when a compromise is permissible and when it is not. He also made out that the way Congress is conducting the movement it was bound to end in some sort of compromise. After analyzing the conditions then prevailing, he finally advised the youth to adopt Marxism as the ideology, work among the people, organize workers and peasants into a party to form the Communist Party.

This document was published in a mutilated form. All references to congress leaders and Soviet Union, Marx, Lenin, and the Communist Party were carefully deleted.]

[In reaction to this self-censorship by national press, Shaheed Sukhdev wrote a letter in which he stated that "We are not repentance for our death what is more painful is the killing of our ideas and views." -ed]

But subsequently, the GOI published it in one of its secret reports in 1936. A photostat copy of the full report is preserved in the library of the Martyrs' Memorial and Freedom Struggle Research Centre at Lucknow.]

Editorial Introduction:

Written on February 2,1931, this document is a sort of behest to young political workers of India. Even while waiting for death penalty, Bhagat Singh was thinking with all clarity about the future of India. He wanted to equip his compatriots with a clear vision and emphasized the principles of achieving the goal of complete independence. His assessment of the national movement at that time is so correct. This document consists of two parts, one, in the form of a letter, followed by notes under the titles: Our Opportunity, Gandhism, Terrorism, Revolution, Programme and Revolutionary Party.

For some time, it has been a puzzle that how it [the document] landed in Bengal. Now we have a first-hand evidence as recorded by Comrade Ram Chandra, the President of *Naujawan Bharat Sabha, in his memoires Naujawan Bharat Sabha and Hindustan Socialist Republican Association/Army* published by author in 1986. Comrade Ram Chandra records (Page 173 of the book) that "Bhagat Singh had written a letter dealing with political situation as it had developed upto that time. This was brought by late Jaswant Singh a silent and noble revolutionary comrade to me.... I handed over this letter to Subash in order to get his total commitment to Naujawan Bharat Sabha. Subash promised to return the letter to me after the Naujawan Session at Karachi (March 25, 1931 along with the Session of National Indian Congress: ed). To keep his word, he searched for me. But as I had been detained at Karachi, he could not return the letter to me. And then it was lost." So, this explains how it reached Calcutta and must have been read by all type of political workers, and was subsequently found in Calcutta.

Mr. CES Fairweather was police commissioner of Kolkata 1939-1943.

This report, along with other police reports of that time, have been since reproduced by the West Bengal Government.

"Terrorism in Bengal"

"Vol 1 A collection of documents on Terrorist Activities from 1905-1939." Ed. Amiya K Samanta-1995

Here is the document as published by Mr. CES Fairweather.]

Secret

Notes on the Development of United Front Movement in Bengal (PAGES 45 to 57)

CES Fairweather   8.9.1936

Revolutionary programme drafted by Bhagat Singh (hanged) and found in the house search of (detenu) Mrs. Bimala Pratibha Devi in Calcutta on 3rd October 1931.

Note: I am publishing this as I am firmly convinced that all the revolutionary forces at present moment are tending to operate on the lines indicated in the programme. We have recently (in intercepted correspondence) had a reference to a "Committee of Action". Under the scheme, the degree of control exercised in the most open fashion and as such a manner that those in control can never be connected with criminal activities.

Mr. CES FAIRWEATHER

Calcutta.
November 1, 1933.

To,
The Young Political Workers,

DEAR COMRADES,

Our movement is passing through a very important phase at present. After a year's fierce struggle, some definite proposals regarding the constitutional reforms have been formulated by the Round Table Conference and the Congress leaders have been invited to give this[*] think it desirable in the present circumstances to call off their movement. Whether they decide in favour or against is a matter of little importance to us. The present movement is bound to end in some sort of compromise. The compromise may be effected sooner or later. And compromise is not such ignoble and deplorable a thing as we generally think. It is rather an indispensable factor in the political strategy. Any nation that rises against

---
[*] Some words are missing from the original text.

the oppressors is bound to fail in the beginning, and to gain partial reforms during the medieval period of its struggle through compromises. And it is only at the last stage—having fully organized all the forces and resources of the nation—that it can possibly strike the final blow in which it might succeed to shatter the ruler's government. But even then it might fail, which makes some sort of compromise inevitable. This can be best illustrated by the Russian example.

In 1905, a revolutionary movement broke out in Russia. All the leaders were very hopeful. Lenin had returned from the foreign countries where he had taken refuge. He was conducting the struggle. People came to tell him that a dozen landlords were killed and a score of their mansions were burnt. Lenin responded by telling them to return and to kill 1,200 landlords and burn as many of their palaces. In his opinion that would have meant something if revolution failed. Duma was introduced. The same Lenin advocated the view of participating in the Duma. This is what happened in 1907. In 1906, he was opposed to the participation in this first Duma which had granted more scope of work than this second one whose rights had been curtailed. This was due to the changed circumstances. Reaction was gaining the upper hand and Lenin wanted to use the floor of the Duma as a platform to discuss socialist ideas.

Again after the 1917 revolution, when the Bolsheviks were forced to sign the Brest Litovsk Treaty, everyone except Lenin was opposed to it. But Lenin said: "Peace. Peace, and again, peace: peace at any cost—even at the cost of many of the Russian provinces to be yielded to German War Lord". When some anti-Bolshevik people condemned Lenin for this treaty, he declared frankly that the Bolsheviks were not in a position to face the German onslaught and they preferred the treaty to the complete annihilation of the Bolshevik Government.

The thing that I wanted to point out was that compromise is an essential weapon which has to be wielded every now and then as the struggle develops. But the thing that we must keep always before us is the ideal of the movement. We must always maintain a clear notion as to the aim for the achievement of which we are fighting. That helps us to verify the success and failures of our movements and we can easily formulate the future programme. Tilak's policy, quite apart from the ideal, i.e., his strategy, was the best. You are fighting to get sixteen annas from your enemy, you get only one anna. Pocket it and fight for the rest. What we note in the moderates is of their ideal. They start to achieve one anna and they can't get it. The revolutionaries must always keep in mind that they are striving for a complete revolution. Complete mastery of power in their hands. Compromises are dreaded because the conservatives try to disband the revolutionary forces after the compromise. But able and bold revolutionary leaders can save the movement from such pitfalls. We must be very careful at such junctures to avoid any sort of confusion of the real issues especially the goal. The British Labour leaders betrayed their real struggle and have been reduced to mere hypocrite imperialists. In my opinion, the diehard conservatives are better to us than these polished imperialist Labour leaders. About the tactics and strategy one should study life-work of Lenin. His definite views on the subject of compromise will be found in "Left-Wing Communism."

I have said that the present movement, i.e., the present struggle, is bound to end in some sort of compromise or complete failure.

I said that, because in my opinion, this time the real revolutionary forces have not been invited into the arena. This is a struggle dependent upon the middle-class shopkeepers and a few capitalists. Both these, and particularly the latter, can never dare to risk its property or possessions in any struggle. The real revolutionary armies are in the villages and in factories, the peasantry and the labourers. But our bourgeois leaders do not and cannot dare to tackle them. The sleeping lion once awakened from its slumber shall become irresistible even after the achievement of what our leaders aim at. After his first experience with the Ahmedabad labourers in 1920, Mahatma Gandhi declared: "We must not tamper with the labourers. It is dangerous to make political use of the factory proletariat" (*The Times*, May 1921). Since then, they never dared to approach them. There remains the peasantry. The Bardoli resolution of 1922 clearly defines the horror the leaders felt when they saw the gigantic peasant class rising to shake off not only the domination of an alien nation but also the yoke of the landlords.

It is there that our leaders prefer a surrender to the British than to the peasantry. Leave alone Pt. Jawahar Lal. Can you point out any effort to organize the peasants or the labourers? No, they will not run the risk. There they lack. That is why I say they never meant a complete revolution. Through economic and administrative pressure, they hoped to get a few more reforms, a few more concessions for the Indian capitalists. That is why I say that this movement is doomed to die, may be after some sort of compromise or even without. They young workers who in all sincerity raise the cry "Long Live Revolution", are not well organized and strong enough to carry the movement themselves. As a matter of fact, even our great leaders, with the exception of perhaps Pt. Motilal Nehru, do not dare to take any responsibility on their shoulders, that is why every now and then they surrender unconditionally before Gandhi. In spite of their differences, they never oppose him seriously and the resolutions have to be carried for the Mahatma.

In these circumstances, let me warn the sincere young workers who seriously mean a revolution, that harder times are coming. Let them beware lest they should get confused or disheartened. After the experience made through two struggles of the Great Gandhi, we are in a better position to form a clear idea of our present position and the future programme.

Now allow me to state the case in the simplest manner. You cry "Long Live Revolution." Let me assume that you really mean it. According to our definition of the term, as stated in our statement in the Assembly Bomb Case, revolution means complete overthrow of the existing social order and its replacement with the socialist order. For that purpose, our immediate aim is the achievement of power. As a matter of fact, the state, the government machinery is just a weapon in the hands of the ruling class to further and safeguard its interest. We want to snatch and handle it to utilise it for the consummation of our ideal, i.e., social reconstruction on new, i.e., Marxist, basis. For this purpose, we are fighting to handle the government machinery. All along we have to educate the masses to create a favourable atmosphere for our social programme. In the struggles we can best train and educate them.

With these things clear before us, i.e., our immediate and ultimate object having been clearly put, we can now proceed with the examination of the present situation. We must always be very candid and quite business-like while analyzing any situation.

We know that since a hue and cry was raised about the Indians' participation in and share in the responsibility of the Indian government, the Minto-Morley Reforms were introduced, which formed the Viceroy's council with consultation rights only. During the Great War, when the Indian help was needed the most, promises about self-government were made and the existing reforms were introduced. Limited legislative powers have been entrusted to the Assembly but subject to the goodwill of the Viceroy. Now is the third stage.

Now reforms are being discussed and are to be introduced in the near future. How can our young men judge them? This is a question; I do not know by what standard are the Congress leaders going to judge them. But for us, the revolutionaries, we can have the following criteria:

1. Extent of responsibility transferred to the shoulders of the Indians.

2. From of the government institutions that are going to be introduced and the extent of the right of participation given to the masses.

3. Future prospects and the safeguards.

These might require a little further elucidation. In the first place, we can easily judge the extent of responsibility given to our people by the control our representatives will have on the executive. Up till now, the executive was never made responsible to the Legislative Assembly and the Viceroy had the veto power, which rendered all the efforts of the elected members futile. Thanks to the efforts of the

Swaraj Party, the Viceroy was forced every now and then to use these extraordinary powers to shamelessly trample the solemn decisions of the national representatives under foot. It is already too well known to need further discussion.

Now in the first place we must see the method of the executive formation: Whether the executive is to be elected by the members of a popular assembly or is to be imposed from above as before, and further, whether it shall be responsible to the house or shall absolutely affront it as in the past?

As regards the second item, we can judge it through the scope of franchise. The property qualifications making a man eligible to vote should be altogether abolished and universal suffrage be introduced instead. Every adult, both male and female, should have the right to vote. At present we can simply see how far the franchise has been extended.

I may here make a mention about provincial autonomy. But from whatever I have heard, I can only say that the Governor imposed from above, equipped with extraordinary powers, higher and above the legislative, shall prove to be no less than a despot. Let us better call it the "provincial tyranny" instead of "autonomy". This is a strange type of democratization of the state institutions.

The third item is quite clear. During the last two years, the British politicians have been trying to undo Montagu's promise for another dole of reforms to be bestowed every ten years till the British Treasury exhausts.

We can see what they have decided about the future.

Let me make it clear that we do not analyze these things to rejoice over the achievement, but to form a clear idea about our situation, so that we may enlighten the masses and prepare them for further struggle. For us, compromise never means surrender, but a step forward and some rest. That is all and nothing else.

◻

Having discussed the present situation, let us proceed to discuss the future programme and the line of action we ought to adopt.

As I have already stated, for any revolutionary party a definite programme is very essential. For, you must know that revolution means action. It means a change brought about deliberately by an organized and systematic work, as opposed to sudden and unorganized or spontaneous change or breakdown. And for the formulation of a programme, one must necessarily study:

1. The goal.

2. The premises from where we are to start, i.e., the existing conditions.

3. The course of action, i.e., means and methods.

Unless one has a clear notion about these three factors, one cannot discuss anything about programme.

We have discussed the present situation to some extent. The goal also has been slightly touched. We want a socialist revolution, the indispensable preliminary to which is the political revolution. That is what we want. The political revolution does not mean the transfer of state (or more crudely, the power) from the hands of the British to the Indian, but to those Indians who are at one with us as to the final goal, or to be more precise, the power to be transferred to the revolutionary party through popular support. After that, to proceed in right earnest is to organize the reconstruction of the whole society on the socialist basis. If you do not mean this revolution, then please have mercy. Stop shouting "Long Live Revolution." The term revolution is too sacred, at least to us, to be so lightly used or misused. But if you say you are for the national revolution and the aims of your struggle is an Indian republic of the type of the United State of America, then I ask you to please let me know on what forces you rely that will help you bring about that revolution. The only forces on which you can rely to bring about that revolution whether national or the socialist, are the peasantry and the labour. Congress leaders do not dare to organize those forces. You have seen it in this movement. They know it better than anybody else that without these forces they are absolutely helpless. When they passed the resolution of complete independence—that really meant a revolution—they did not mean it. They had to do it under pressure of the younger element, and then they wanted to use it as a threat to achieve their hearts' desire—Dominion Status. You can easily judge it by studying the resolutions of the last three sessions of the Congress. I mean Madras, Calcutta, and Lahore. At Calcutta, they passed a resolution asking for Dominion Status within 12 months, otherwise they would be forced to adopt complete independence as their object, and in all solemnity waited for some such gift till midnight after the December 31, 1929. Then they found themselves "honour-bound" to adopt the Independence resolution, otherwise they did not mean it. But even then Mahatma Ji made no secret of the fact that the door (for compromise) was open. That was the real spirit. At the very outset they knew that their movement could not but end in some compromise. It is this half-heartedness that we hate, not the compromise at a particular stage in the struggle. Anyway, we were discussing the forces on which you can depend for a revolution. But if you say that you will approach the peasants and labourers to enlist their active support, let me tell you that they are not going to be fooled by any sentimental talk. They ask you quite candidly: what are they going to gain by your revolution for which you demand their sacrifices, what difference does it make to them whether Lord Reading is the head of the Indian government or Sir Purshotamdas Thakordas? What difference for a peasant if Sir Tej Bahadur Sapru replaces Lord Irwin! It is useless to appeal to his national sentiment. You can't "use" him for your purpose; you shall have to mean seriously and to make him understand that the revolution is going to be his and for his good. The revolution of the proletariat and for the proletariat.

When you have formulated this clear-cut idea about your goals, you can proceed in right earnest to organize your forces for such an action. Now, there are two different phases through which you shall have to pass. First, the preparation; second, the action.

After the present movement ends, you will find disgust and some disappointment amongst the sincere revolutionary workers. But you need not worry. Leave sentimentalism aside. Be prepared to face the facts. Revolution is a very difficult task. It is beyond the power of any man to make a revolution. Neither can it be brought about on any appointed date. It is brought can it be brought about on an appointed date. It is brought about by special environments, social and economic. The function of an organized party is to utilise any such opportunity offered by these circumstances. And to prepare the masses and organize the forces for the revolution is a very difficult task. And that requires a very great sacrifice on the part of the revolutionary workers. Let me make it clear that if you are a businessman or an established worldly or family man, please don't play with fire. As a leader you are of no use to the party. We have already very many such leaders who spare some evening hours for delivering speeches. They are useless. We require—to use the term so dear to Lenin—the "professional revolutionaries". The whole-time workers who have no other ambitions or life-work except the revolution. The greater the number of such workers organized into a party, the greater the chances of your success.

To proceed systematically, what you need the most is a party with workers of the type discussed above with clear-cut ideas and keen perception and ability of initiative and quick decisions. The party shall have iron discipline and it need not necessarily be an underground party, rather the contrary. Though the policy of voluntarily going to jail should altogether be abandoned. That will create a number of workers who shall be forced to lead an underground life. They should carry on the work with the same zeal. And it is this group of workers that shall produce worthy leaders for the real opportunity.

The party requires workers which can be recruited only through the youth movement. Hence we find the youth movement as the starting point of our programme. The youth movement should organize study circles, class lectures and publication of leaflets, pamphlets, books and periodicals. This is the best recruiting and training ground for political workers.

Those young men who may have matured their ideas and may find themselves ready to devote their life to the cause, may be transferred to the party. The party workers shall always guide and control the work of the youth movement as well. The party should start with the work of mass propaganda. It is very essential. One of the fundamental causes of the failure of the efforts of the Ghadar Party (1914-15) was the ignorance, apathy and sometimes active opposition of the masses. And apart from that, it is essential for gaining the active sympathy of and organizing the peasants and workers. The name of party or rather, a communist party. This party of political workers, bound by strict discipline, should handle all other movements. It shall have to organize the peasants' and workers' parties, labour unions, and may even venture to capture the Congress and kindred political bodies. And in order to create political consciousness, not only of national politics but class politics as well as the party should organize a big publishing campaign. Subjects on all proletarians enlightening the masses of the socialist theory shall be within easy reach and distributed widely. The writings should be simple and clear.

There are certain people in the labour movement who enlist some absurd ideas about the economic liberty of the peasants and workers without political freedom. They are demagogues or muddle-headed people. Such ideas are unimaginable and preposterous. We mean the economic liberty of the masses, and for that very purpose we are striving to win the political power. No doubt in the beginning, we shall have to fight for little economic demands and privileges of these classes. But these struggles are the best means for educating them for a final struggle to conquer political power.

Apart from these, there shall necessarily be organized a military department. This is very important. At times its need is felt very badly. But at that time you cannot start and formulate such a group with substantial means to act effectively. Perhaps this is the topic that needs a careful explanation. There is very great probability of my being misunderstood on this subject. Apparently, I have acted like a terrorist. But I am not a terrorist. I am a revolutionary who has got such definite ideas of a lengthy programme as is being discussed here. My "comrades in arms" might accuse me, like Ram Prasad Bismil, for having been subjected to certain sort of reaction in the condemned cell, which is not true. I have got the same ideas, same convictions, same zeal and same spirit as I used to have outside, perhaps-nay, decidedly-better. Hence, I warn my readers to be careful while reading my words. They should not try to read anything between the lines. Let me announce with all the strength at my command, that I am not a terrorist and I never was, expect perhaps in the beginning of my revolutionary career. And I am convinced that we cannot gain anything through those methods. One can easily judge it from the history of the Hindustan Socialist Republican Association. All our activities were directed towards an aim, i.e., identifying ourselves with the great movement as its military wing. If anybody has misunderstood me, let him amend his ideas. I do not mean that bombs and pistols are useless, rather the contrary. But I mean to say that mere bomb-throwing is not only useless but sometimes harmful. The military department of the party should always keep ready all the war material it can command for any emergency. It should back the political work of the party. It cannot and should not work independently.

On these lines indicated above, the party should proceed with its work. Through periodical meetings and conferences, they should go on educating and enlightening their workers on all topics.

If you start the work on these lines, you shall have to be very sober. The programme requires at least twenty years for its fulfilment. Cast aside the youthful dreams of a revolution within ten years of Gandhi's utopian promises of Swaraj in one year. It requires neither the emotion nor the death, but the life of constant struggle, suffering, and sacrifice. Crush your individuality first. Shake off the dreams of personal comfort. Then start to work. Inch by inch you shall have to proceed. It needs courage, perseverance and very strong determination. No difficulties and no hardships shall discourage you. No failure and betrayals shall dishearten you. No travails imposed upon you shall snuff out the revolutionary zeal in you. Through the ordeal of sufferings and sacrifice you shall come out victorious. And these individual victories shall be the valuable assets of the revolution.

LONG LIVE REVOLUTION!
February 2, 1931

OUR OPPORTUNITY

Indian freedom is not perhaps any longer a far distant dream; events are moving apace and it may become a reality sooner than we expect. British Imperialism is admittedly in a tight corner. Germany is about to topple down, France is tottering, even the United States shaky. And their difficulty is our opportunity. Everything points to that long prophesied eventuality—the ultimate and inevitable breakdown of the capitalistic order of society. Diplomats may agree to save themselves and capitalistic conspiracy may yet keep wolf of revolution away from their doors. The British budget may be balanced, the moribund mark granted some hours of respite and King Dollar may retain his crown; but the trade depression if continued and continued it must be, we know the members of unemployed being multiplied daily as a result of the capitalistic race in production and competition is bound to throw the capitalistic system out of gear in the months to come. The revolution is, therefore, no longer a prophecy and prospect—but "practical politics" for thoughtful planning and remorseless execution. Let there be no confusion of thought as to its aspect or as to its immediacy, its methods, and its objective.

GANDHISM

We should not have any illusion about the possibilities, failures, and achievements of Congress movement, which should be, as it is today, be better stamped Gandhism. It does not stand for freedom avowedly; it is in favour of "parternership"—a strange interpretation of what "complete independence" signifies. Its method is novel, and but for the helplessness of the people. Gandhism would gain no adherent for the Saint of Sabarmati. It has fulfilled and is fulfilling the role of an intermediate party of liberal-radical combination fighting shy of reality of the situation and controlled mostly by men with stakes in the country, who prize their stakes with bourgeois tenacity, and it is bound to stagnate unless rescued from its own fate by an infusion of revolutionary blood. It must be saved from its friends.

TERRORISM

Let us be clear on this thorny question of terrorism. The cult of the bomb is old as 1905 and it is a sad comment on revolutionary India that they have not yet realized its use and misuse. Terrorism is a confession that the revolutionary mentality has not penetrated down into the masses. It is thus a confession of our failure. In the initial stages, it had its use; it shook the torpor out of body politic, enkindled the imagination of young intelligentsia, fired their spirit of self-sacrifice and demonstrated before the world and before our enemies the truth and the strength of the movement. But by itself it is not enough. Its history is a history of failure in every land—France, in Russia, in Balkan countries, in Germany, in Spain, everywhere. It bears the germ of defeat within itself. The Imperialist knows that to rule 300 million he must sacrifice 30 of his men annually. The pleasure of ruling may be bombed out or pistolled down, but the practical gain from exploitation will make him stick to his post. Even though arms were as readily available as we hope for, and were it be pushed with a thoroughness unknown anywhere else, terrorism can at most force the Imperialist power to come to terms with party. Such terms a little more or less, must fall short of our objective—complete independence. Terrorism thus hope to wring out what Gandhism bids fair to attain—a compromise and an installment of reforms—a replacement of a white rule at Delhi by a brown rule. It is aloof from the life of the masses and once installed on the throne runs the risk of being petrified into a tyranny. The Irish parallel, I have to warn, does not apply in our case. In Ireland, it was not sporadic terroristic activities she witnessed; it was a nationwide rising, the rank and file were bound by an intimate knowledge and sympathy with the gunmen. Arms they could have very easily, and the American–Irish poured out their money. Topography favoured such a warfare, and Ireland after all had to be satisfied with an unaccomplished movement. It has lessened the bonds but not released the Irish proletariat from the shackles of the capitalist, native and foreign. Ireland is a lesson to India and a warning—warning how nationalistic idealism devoid of revolutionary social basis although with all other circumstances in its favor, may (be?) lost itself in the shoals of a compromise with Imperialism. Should India, if she could imitate Ireland still?

In a sense, Gandhism, with its counter-revolutionary creed of quietism, makes a nearer approach to the revolutionary ideas. For it counts on mass action, though not for the masses alone. They have paved the way for the proletariat revolution by trying to harness them, however crudely and selfishly to its political programme. The revolutionary must give to the angle of non-violence his due.

The devil of terrorism needs, however, no compliments. The terrorist has done much, taught us much, and has his use still, provided we do not make a confusion of our aims and means. At desperate moments we can make of terrorist outrages our best publicity works but it is none the less fireworks and should be reserved for a chosen few. Let not the revolutionary be lashed round and round the vicious circle of aimless outrages and individual self-immolation. The inspiring ideal for all and sundry workers should not be that of dying for the cause but of living for the cause, and living usefully and worthily.

Needless to point out, that we do not repudiate terrorist activities altogether. We want to assess its proper value from the standpoint of proletariat revolution. The youth, who is found not to fit in with the cold and silent organization work, has another role to play—he is to be released from the dry work and allowed to fulfill his destiny. But the controlling body should always forsee the possible reaction of the deed on the party, the masses and on the enemy. It may divert the attention of the first two from militant mass action to the stirring sensational action and it may supply to last with clues for striking at the root of the whole party in either case it does not advance the cause.

Secret military organization is, however, not an anathema. Indeed, it is the front line, "the firing line" of the revolutionary party; must be linked with the "base" formed by a mobile and militant mass party. Collections of arms and finances for organization are, therefore, to be undertaken without any scruple.

REVOLUTION

What we mean by revolution is quite plan. In this century it can mean only one thing—the capture of the political power by the masses for the masses. It is, in fact, The Revolution. Other risings attempt a mere change of your lordships, trying to perpetuate the rotting capitalistic order. No amount of profession of sympathy for the people and the popular cause can ultimately hoodwink the masses about the true nature and portent of such superficial replacement. In India, too, we want nothing less than the regime of the Indian proletariat in the place of the Indian Imperialists and their native allies who are barricaded behind the same eronomic system of exploration. We can suffer no black evil to replace the white evil. The evils have a community of interest to do any such thing.

The proletariat revolution is the only weapon of India to dislodge the Imperialist. Nothing else can attain this object. Nationalists of all shades are agreed on the objective—Independence of the Imperialists. They must realize rebelliousness of the masses is the motive force behind their agitation and militant mass action alone can push it to success. Having no recourse to it easily, they always delude themselves with the vision of the what they consider a temporary remedy but quick and effective remedy, viz overthrowing the foreign rule by an armed opposition of a few hundreds of determined idealist nationalists and then reconstructing the State on socialistic lines. They should see into reality of the situation, arms are not plenty, and in the modern world the insurrection of an untrained body isolated from the militant masses stands no chance of success. The nationalists to be effective must harness the nation into action, into revolt. And the nation are not the loudspeakers of the Congress; it is the peasants and the labourers who form more than 95 per cent of India. The nation will stir itself to action only on assurance of nationalization, i.e., freedom from slavery of Imperialist-capitalists.

What we need to keep in mind is that no revolution can succeed or is to be desired, but the proletariat revolution.

THE PROGRAMME

The need of hour is, therefore, for a clear, honest programme for the revolution, and determined action for realization of the programme.

In 1917, before the October Revolution had come off Lenin, still in hiding in Moscow, wrote that for a successful revolution three condition are essential:

1. A political-economic situation.

2. A rebellious mass mind, and,

3. A party of revolutionaries, trained and determined to lead the masses when the hour of trial arrives.

The first condition has been more than fulfilled in India; the second and third yet await finally and completeness. To mobilize them is the work before all workers of freedom and the programme should be farmed with that end in view. We propose to discuss its outline in the following and our suggestion on each section are to be detailed out in the Appendix A and Appendix B.

(1) The base work: The foremost duty before workers is to mobilize the masses for militant mass action. We need not play on blind prejudices, sentiment, piety or passive idealism. Our promises to him are not mere sops or half a loaf. They are complete and concrete, and we can be with him sincere and plain, and should never create in his mind any miasma of prejudices. The revolution is for him, for him to name only the prominent heads:

1. Abolition of landlordism.

2. Liquidation of the peasants' indebtedness.

3. Nationalization of land by the revolutionary state with a view finally to lead to improved and collective farming.

4. Guarantee of security as to housing.

5. Abolition of all charges on the peasantry, except a minimum of unitary land tax.

6. Nationalization of the industries and industrialization of the country.

7. Universal education.

8. Reduction of the hours of work to the minimum necessary.

The masses are bound to respond to such a programme—we have only to reach them. It is the supreme task. Enforced ignorance on their part, and apathy of the intelligent classes on the other, have created an artificial barrier between the educated revolutionary and his less fortunate comrade of the sickle and the hammer. That must be demolished by the revolutionary, and for that purpose:

1. The Congress platform is to be availed of.

2. The trade union are to be captured and new unions and bodies shaped and modelled on aggressive lines.

3. Ryat Union are to be formed to organize them on the issues indicated.

4. Every social and philanthropic organization (even the cooperative societies) that offers an opportunity to approach the masses should be secretly entered into and its activities controlled so as to further the real objective.

5. The unions are committees of artisans workers as well as intellectual workers and are to be set up everywhere.

These are the lines of approach for the educated and trained revolutionary to reach the masses. And once they are reached, they can be moved easily by a training, at first in aggressive assertion of their rights, and later on, by militant offensives like strikes combined with sabotage.

THE REVOLUTIONARY PARTY

It is on the active group of revolutionary that the main task of reaching the masses as well as preparing them for the action rests. They are the mobile, determined mind which will energise the nation into a militant life. As circumstances arise, they come and will also come for sometime longer from the ranks of the revolutionary intelligentsia, who have broken away from their bourgeois or petty bourgeois traditions. The revolutionary party will be composed of these souls and they will gather around them the more and more active recruits from the labour, peasant or small artisan classes. It will be mainly a body of revolutionary—intellectuals, men and women, and on them will devolve the duty of planning and executing, publicity and propaganda, initiating and organizing, or coordinating the activities and linking up the different unions into an offensive, of seducing the army and the police and forming the army of revolution with themselves and these forces, of offering combined and organized armed resistance in the shape of raids and risings, of mobilizing forces for mass insurrection and fearlessly guiding them (that?) when that hour comes. In fact, they are the brains of the movement. Hence, what they will require is character, i.e., capacity for initiative and revolutionary leadership and above all it should be disciplined and strengthened by an intensive study of politics, economic problems, of history and social tendencies, and current diplomatic relations, of the progressive sciences and the science and art of modern warfare. Revolution is the creation of hard thinkers and hard workers. Unfortunately, the intellectual equipment of the Indian revolutionaries is often neglected, but this has made them lose sight of the essential of revolution as well as the proper bearing of their actions. So, a revolutionary must make of his studies a holy duty.

The party, it is clear, can in certain matters act openly and publicly. It should not be secret in so far as it can help it. This will disarm suspicion and will bestow on it prestige and power. The party will have to shoulder high responsibilities, so it will be convenient to divide it into certain committees for every area with special tasks allocated to each of them. The division should be flexible, and according to the needs of the hour or on the study of the possibilities of a member, he should be assigned duties under any such local committee. The local committees are subordinate to the provincial boards, and they in their turn to the Supreme Council. The work of liaison "linking" within the province should be the concern of the P. B and inter-provincial liaison is to be maintained by the Supreme Council. All sporadic actions or disintegrating factors are to be checked but over-centralization is not feasible, and hence, better not be attempted yet.

All the local committees should work in close cooperation having on each one representative of other committee. The committee should be small, composite, and efficient, never allowed to degenerate into discussion clubs.

The local revolutionary party in each area should have:

(a) General Committee: Recruitment, propaganda amongst military, general policy, organization. Co-ordination of the popular Unions (See App. A)

(b) Committee of Finance: This committee may be composed with a majority of women members. On it, rests the most difficult of all takes and, hence, it should have ungrudging help from the others. The sources of finance are: voluntary contribution, forced contribution (government money). Foreign capitalist and banking houses, native one in order of precedence, outrages on private personal wealth (however repugnant to our policy reacts against the party and should not be encouraged), contraband sources (embezzlement).

(c) Committee of action: Its composition—A secret body for sabotage, collection of arms. Training for insurrection.

(d) Groups (a) Younger: Espionage, local military survey (b) Experts: collection of arms, military training etc.

(e) Committee of Women: Though no artificial barrier is recognized between men and women, yet for the sake of convenience and safety of the party, there should be for the time being, such a body entirely responsible for its own members. They may be put in entire charge of the (b) F. C. and of the considerable activities of the (a) G. C. Their scope on (c) is very limited. Their primary duties will be to revolutionize the women folk and select from them active members for direct service.

It might be concluded from the programme outlined that there is no short cut to revolution or freedom. It cannot "dawn on us one fine morning". That would, were it possible, be a sad day. Without the base work, without the militant masses and the party ready in every way, it would be a failure. So, we have to stir ourselves. And we have to remember all the time that the capitalistic order is drifting ahead for a disaster—the catastrophe will come off perhaps, in course of two or three years. And if we still dissipate our energies or do not mobilize the revolutionary forces, the crisis will come and find us wanting. Let us be warned and accept two and three years plan of revolution.

APPENDIX A.

Duties of the General Committee.

Recruiting groups: A country-wide youth league chain which is almost complete. It has to be linked together and most closely co-operate with the other schools, colleges, gymnasiums, clubs, libraries, study circles, welfare associations and even ashrams—every inch of it are to be nabbed by the youth movement.

Propaganda

The press is the best medium, but in rural areas, the platform is to be utilized. Nothing is so helpful for workers and the masses as cheap, plainly written periodicals, books or leaflets. A warning is to be given against the present supply—the stuff we consume. It is not an easy art to say what one has to say and make other hear him. Special duty of seducing the military should be assigned to tried workers, e.g., 27 per cent of the army of the Punjabi Musalman are to be tampered by their Punjabi kinsmen. The Gurkhas are a problem, the Sikhs, Marhattas, and Rajputs are not so.

General policy

Substitution of the bureaucratic authority by that of the masses. The Union of labourers, ryots, artisans, in their aggressive struggle to enforce their own right must be trained for the revolutionary offensive for capture of the political power.

Co-ordination

Calling for representatives of the local union, to from the local general committees, calling for representatives to form the central committee of the party, and for delegates from time to time to meet in conferences for deciding on policy or programme.

Organization

Besides the forgoing, the selection of the personal and members of other committees.

APPENDIX B.

Duties of the Committee of Action

Two classes of members (1) Junior and Women (ii) Senior. It is to be in charge of the underground work.

(1) Composition: Its membership is bound to be not large but efficient. It should insist on a rigorous discipline. It will supply the leaders for the Revolutionary "Red" Army, hence, extreme care and caution should be taken in its composition, and its existence and activities are to be kept secret from the ordinary members of the party.

Duty of the Junior and Women

(1) Espionage and intelligence supply (2) Collection of Arms; to the present method should be added the method of direct acquisition through international sources; (3) Members should be a sent to Western countries for the purpose and for learning the use of arms, e.g., Lewis and Vickers guns, preparation of hand-grenades, etc.; (4) Action-Survey of the locality. (The government maps are to be spotted showing routes, canals, possible shelters for members.) The model is indicated below from "Field notes, Afghanistan, 1914.")

Chapter

I. Physical features, general boundary, rivers, flood seasons, bridges, forts and ferries, navigability, waistes.

II. Populations, religion, language, tribes, castes, distinctive dress and character.

III. Supply—Fodder, firewood, grain transport, ponies, mules, bullocks, donkeys, horses, camels, motors and buses.

IV. Forces—police, military police—Military their strength, their activities if tempered, Outpost stations, cantonments. Distribution of police, of the military police, of the infantry, cavalry, or artillery—of arms and magazines, guns, pistols, rifles, small arms, and big arms . Possible fighting men from the locality—hostile and friendly.

Roads: Description and a chart as follow
1. From ____ to____ Miles
2. Stages:____ stop____ Miles
5. Nature: Metalled—Motorable—Kutcha, etc.
6. Obstacles: Difficult in rains, etc.
7. Water supply, fuel, fodder connection, with remarks.

Training in volunteer corps—University corps, etc. Thorough study of the Field Service Regulation (Vol. I And Vol. II) is bound to be profitable. This knowledge is essential. Study of more military literature and acquaintance with wherever possible. Soldiers in barracks and cantons to be encouraged.

Duty of the Seniors

Action of Finance: To be undertaken at the request of F.C and G.C with their sanction. To be limited to public money and foreign capitalistic gains for the present. The effect on popularity and unpopularity should be final test for such action.

SABOTAGE

On behalf of the Unions at the direction of G.C.

COLLECTION OF ARMS

See foregoing.

ACTIONS FOR TERRRORISING

Against individual only in very extreme cases when his offence is against the public, not against mere groups or individual. Generally, to be discouraged unless forged circumstances.

INSURRECTION

When the Supreme Council directs. Group rising essential. Raids for arms.

23

"We Are War Prisoners, Shoot Us, Do Not Hang Us!"
Bhagat Singh's Last Petition Letter to the Governor of Punjab, Shimla (March, 1931)

Bhagat Singh wrote this letter (three days prior to their execution) while he was in Lahore Central Jail where they (Bhagat Singh, Sukhdev Thapar, and Shivaram Rajguru) were sentenced to death for killing junior British police officer John Saunders. This letter was written with a demand that they be treated as 'war prisoners' and be shot dead instead of being hanged.

To:

The Punjab Governor
Sir,

With due respect we beg to bring to your kind notice the following:

That we were sentenced to death on October 7, 1930 by a British Court, L.C.C. Tribunal, constituted under the Sp. Lahore Conspiracy Case Ordinance, promulgated by the H.E. The Viceroy, the Head of the British Government of India, and that the main charge against us was that of having waged war against H.M. King George, the King of England.

The above-mentioned finding of the Court pre-supposed two things:

Firstly, that there exists a state of war between the British Nation and the Indian Nation, and secondly, that we had actually participated in that war and were, therefore, war prisoners.

The second pre-supposition seems to be a little bit flattering, but nevertheless it is too tempting to resist the desire of acquiescing in it.

As regards the first, we are constrained to go into some detail. Apparently, there seems to be no such war as the phrase indicates. Nevertheless, please allow us to accept the validity of the pre-supposition taking it at its face value. But in order to be correctly understood we must explain it further. Let us declare that the state of war does exist and shall exist so long as the Indian toiling masses and the natural resources are being exploited by a handful of parasites. They may be purely British Capitalist or mixed British and Indian or even purely Indian. They may be carrying on their insidious exploitation through mixed or even on purely Indian bureaucratic apparatus. All these things make no difference. No matter, if your government tries and succeeds in winning over the leaders of the upper strata of the Indian Society through petty concessions and compromises and thereby cause a temporary demoralization in the main body of the forces. No matter, if, once again, the vanguard of the Indian movement, the Revolutionary Party, finds itself deserted in the thick of the war. No matter, if the leaders to whom personally we are much indebted for the sympathy and feelings they expressed for us, but nevertheless we cannot overlook the fact that they did become so callous as to ignore and not to make a mention in the peace negotiation of even the homeless, friendless, and penniless of female workers who are alleged to be belonging to the vanguard and whom the leaders consider to be enemies of their utopian non-violent cult which has already become a thing of the past; the heroines who had ungrudgingly sacrificed or offered for sacrifice their husbands, brothers, and all that were nearest and dearest to them, including themselves, whom your government has declared to be outlaws. No matter, if your agents stoop so low as to fabricate baseless calumnies against their spotless characters to damage their and their party's reputation. The war shall continue.

It may assume different shapes at different times. It may become now open, now hidden, now purely agitational, now fierce life, and death struggle. The choice of the course, whether bloody or comparatively peaceful, which it should adopt rests with you. Choose whichever you like. But that war shall be incessantly waged without taking into consideration the petty (illegible) and the meaningless ethical ideologies. It shall be waged ever with new vigour, greater audacity and unflinching determination till the Socialist Republic is established and the present social order is completely replaced by a new social order, based on social prosperity and thus every sort of exploitation is put an end to, and the humanity is ushered into the era of genuine and permanent peace. In the very near future, the final battle shall be fought and final settlement arrived at.

The days of capitalist and imperialist exploitation are numbered. The war neither began with us nor is it going to end with our lives. It is the inevitable consequence of the historic events and the existing environments. Our humble sacrifices shall be only a link in the chain that has very accurately been beautified by the unparalleled sacrifice of Mr. Das and most tragic but noblest sacrifice of Comrade Bhagawati Charan and the glorious death of our dear warrior Azad.

As to the question of our fates, please allow us to say that when you have decided to put us to death, you will certainly do it. You have got the power in your hands and the power is the greatest justification in this world. We know that the maxim "Might is right" serves as your guiding motto. The whole of our trial was just a proof of that. We wanted to point out that according to the verdict of your court, we had waged war and were, therefore, war prisoners. And we claim to be treated as such, i.e., we claim to be shot dead instead of to be hanged. It rests with you to prove that you really meant what your court has said.

We request and hope that you will very kindly order the military department to send its detachment to perform our execution.

Yours,
Bhagat Singh

24

"Mr. Kishan's Action Was Part of the Struggle Itself"
Bhagat Singh on the Line of Defence in Hari Kishan's Case
(June, 1931)

On December 23, 1930, as the British Governor of Punjab Sir Geoffrey de Montmorency was exiting the University Hall, Lahore, after delivering his convocation address, Hari Kishan, a young revolutionary, fired at him. One man died and the Governor was slightly injured. During the trial, Hari Kishan's defence counsel took the line of defence stating that Hari Kishan had no intention to kill the Governor and that he only wanted to give a warning. Bhagat Singh was opposed to this line of defence. He wrote to one of his friends about how revolutionary cases should be conducted. This letter was published in *The People* in June 1931.

I am very sorry to note that my last letter in this connection did not reach its destination at the proper time and, therefore, could be of no use, or failed to serve the purpose or which it was written. Hence, I write this letter to let you know my views on the question of defence in the political cases in general and the revolutionary cases in particular. Apart from certain points already discussed in that letter, it shall serve another purpose too, i.e., it shall be a documentary proof that I am not becoming wise after the event.

Anyhow, I wrote in that letter that the plea that the lawyer was suggesting to offer defence, should not be adopted. But it has been done in spite of your, and my, opposition. Nevertheless, we can now discuss the matter in a better light and can formulate definite ideas about the future policy regarding defence.

You know that I have never been in favour of defending all the political accused. But this does not imply that the beauty of the real struggle should be spoiled altogether. (Please note that the term "beauty" is not used in the abstract sense but it means the motive that actuated a particular action). When I say that all the politicals should always defend themselves, I say it with certain reservations. It can be cleared by just one explanation. A man does an act with a certain end in view. After his arrest, the political significance of the action should not be diminished. The perpetrator should not become more important than the action itself. Let us further elucidate it with the help of the illustration. Mr. Hari Kishan came to shoot the Governor. I don't want only to discuss the ethical side of the action. I want only to discuss the political side of the case. The man was arrested. Unfortunately, some police official died in the action as well. Now, comes the question of the defence; well, when fortunately the Governor had escaped, there could be a very beautiful statement in his case, i.e., the statement of actual facts as it was made in the lower court. And it would have served the legal purpose, too. The wisdom and ability of the lawyer depended on his interpretation of the cause of the Sub-Inspector's death. What did he gain by saying that he did not intend to kill the Governor and only wanted to warn him, and all that sort of thing? Can any sensible man imagine even for a moment the possibility of such a design? Had it any legal value? Absolutely none. Then, what was the use of spoiling the beauty of not only the particular action but also the general movement? Warning and futile protests cannot go on forever. The warning has once been given long ago. The revolutionary struggle had begun in right earnest so far as the strength of the revolutionary party allowed. Viceroy's train action was neither a test nor a warning. Similarly, Mr. Hari Kishan's action was part of the struggle itself, not a warning. After the failure of the action, the accused can take it in purely sportsman-like spirit. The purpose having been served, he ought to have rejoiced in the lucky escape of the Governor. There is no use of killing any one individual. These actions have their political significance in as much as they serve to create a mentality and an atmosphere which shall be very necessary to the final struggle. That is all. Individual actions are to win the moral support of the people. We sometimes designate them as the 'propaganda through deed'.

Now, the people should be defended but subject to the above consideration. This is, after all, a common principle that all the contending parties always try to gain more and to lose less. No general can ever adopt a policy in which he may have to make a greater sacrifice than the gain expected. Nobody would be more anxious to save the precious life of Mr. Hari Kishan than myself. But I want to let you know that the thing which makes his life precious should by no means be ignored. To save the lives at any cost, is not our policy. It may be the policy of the easy-chair politicians, but it is not ours.

Much of the defence policy depends upon the mentality of the accused himself. But if the accused himself is not only afraid of shrinking but is as enthusiastic as ever, than his work for which he risked his life should be considered first, his personal question afterwards. Again, there may be some sort of confusion. There may be cases where the action is of no general importance in spite of its tremendous local value. There the accused should not be sentimental as to admit the responsibility. The famous trial of Nirmal Kant Rai would be the best illustration.

But in cases like this, where it is of such political importance, the personal aspect should not be attached greater value than the political one. If you want to know my frank opinion about his case, let me tell you frankly that it is nothing short of the political murder of an incident of historic importance at the altar of professional (legal) vanity.

Here, I may point out one more thing, that the people responsible for this strangulation of the case, having realized their blunder and having become wise after the event in not daring to shoulder their responsibility, are trying to belittle the beauty of the marvelous character of our young comrade. I have heard them saying that Mr. Hari Kishan shirked to face it boldly.

This is a most shamefaced lie. He is the most courageous lad I have ever come across. People should have mercy upon us. Better ignored than demoralized and degraded but well looked after.

Lawyers should not be so unscrupulous as to exploit the lives and even deaths of young people who come to sacrifice themselves for so noble a cause as the emancipation of the suffering humanity. I am really...*, Otherwise, why should a lawyer demand such an incredible fee as has been paid in the above case?

In the sedition cases, I may tell you the limit to which we can allow the defence. Last year, when one comrade was prosecuted for having delivered a socialistic speech and when he pleaded not guilty to that charge, we were simply astounded. In such cases, we should demand the right of free speech. But where such things are attributed to one as he has not said and are contrary to the interests of the movement, deny. Though in the present movement the Congress has suffered for having allowed its members to go to jail without defending themselves, in my opinion, that was a mistake.

---

* Some text missing from the original text.

Anyhow, I think if you read this letter along with my previous one, you will come to know very clearly my ideas about the defence in political cases. In Mr. Hari Kishan's case, in my opinion, his appeal should be filed in the High Court without fail and every effort should be made to save him.

I hope both these letters indicate everything I want to say on this subject.

25

Introduction to Dreamland

Lala Ram Saran Das, a Ghadar Party revolutionary involved in the Ghadar Mutiny, was convicted for life in 1915 in the first Lahore Conspiracy Case. While in Salem Central Prison, Madras Presidency, he wrote a book of poems titled *The Dreamland*. After his release in the mid-twenties, he contacted Bhagat Singh and Sukhdev and became an active member of the Hindustan Socialist Republican Association. He was arrested again in connection with the second Lahore Conspiracy Case. This time he wavered and accepted king's pardon. Soon he realized the mistake and retracted his statement. He was charged of perjury and convicted for two years which was subsequently reduced to six months in appeal. It was during this conviction that he passed on his manuscript to Bhagat Singh for an introduction.

In this introduction, while appreciating the spirit behind Ram Saran Das's work, Bhagat Singh has criticized his utopian approach to the problems of revolution. He has also expressed himself on subjects such as God, religion, violence and non-violence, spiritualism, literature, poetry, etc.

My noble friend, L. Ram Saran Das, has asked me to write an introduction to his poetical work, *'The Dreamland'*. I am neither a poet nor a littérateur, neither am I a journalist nor a critic. Hence, by no stretch of imagination can I find the justification of the demand. But the circumstances in which I am placed do not afford any opportunity of discussing the question with the author arguing back and forth, and thereby do not leave me any alternative but to comply with the desire of my friend.

As I am not a poet I am not going to discuss it from that point of view. I have absolutely no knowledge of metre, and do not even know whether judged from metrical standard it would prove correct. Not being a littérateur I am not going to discuss it with a view of assigning to it its right place in the national literature.

I, being a political worker, can at the utmost discuss it only from that point of view. But here also one factor is making my work practically impossible or at least very difficult. As a rule, the introduction is always written by a man who is at one with the author on the contents of the work. But, here the case a quite different. I do not see eye to eye with my friend on all the matters. He was aware of the fact that I differed from him on many vital points. Therefore, my writing is not going to be an introduction at all. It can at the utmost amount to a criticism, and its place will be at the end and not in the beginning of the book.

In the political field, *The Dreamland* occupies a very important place. In the prevailing circumstance it is filling up a very important gap in the movement. As a matter of fact, all the political movements of our country that have hitherto played any important role in our modern history, had been lacking the ideal at the achievement of which they aimed. Revolutionary movement is no exception. In spite of all my efforts, I could not find any revolutionary party that had clear ideas as to what they were fighting for, with the exception of the Ghadar Party, which, having been inspired by the USA form of government, clearly stated that they wanted to replace the existing government by a Republican form of government. All other parties consisted of men who had but one idea, i.e., to fight against the alien rulers. That idea is quite laudable but cannot be termed a revolutionary idea. We must make it clear that revolution does not merely mean an upheaval or a sanguinary strife. Revolution necessarily implies the programme of systematic reconstruction of society on new and better adapted basis, after complete destruction of the existing state of affairs (i.e., regime).

In the political field the liberals wanted some reform under the present government, while the extremists demanded a bit more and were prepared to employ radical means for the same purpose. Among the revolutionaries, they had always been in favour of extreme methods with one idea, i.e., to overthrow the foreign domination. No doubt, there had been some who were in favour of extorting some reforms through those means. All these movements cannot rightly be designated as revolutionary movement.

But L. Ram Saran Das is the first revolutionary recruited formally in the Punjab by a Bengali absconder in 1908. Since then he had been in touch with the revolutionary movements and finally joined the Ghadar Party but retaining his old ideas that people held about the ideal of their movement. It has another interesting fact to add to its beauty and value. L. Ram Saran Das was sentenced to death in 1915, and the sentence was later on commuted to life transportation. Today, sitting in the condemned cells myself, I can let the readers know as authoritatively that the life imprisonment is comparatively a far harder lot than that of death. L. Ram Saran Das had to actually undergo 14 years of imprisonment. It was in some southern jail that he wrote this poetry. The then psychology and mental struggle of the author has stamped its impressions upon the poetry and makes it all the more beautiful and interesting. He had been struggling hard against some depressing mood before he had decided to write. In the days when many of his comrades had been let off on undertakings and the temptation had been very strong for everyone and for him, too, and when the sweet and painful memories of wife and children had added more to the work. Hence, we find the sudden outburst in the opening paragraph:

"Wife, children, friends that me surround
Were poisonous snakes all around."

He discusses philosophy in the beginning. This philosophy is the backbone of all the revolutionary movement of Bengal as well as of the Punjab. I differ from him on this point very widely. His interpretation of the universe is teleological and metaphysical, which I am a materialist and my interpretation of the phenomenon would be causal. Nevertheless, it is by no means out of place or out of date. The general ideal that are prevailing in our country, are more in accordance with those expressed by him. To fight that depressing mood he resorted to prayers as is evident that the whole of the beginning of the book is devoted to God, His praise, His definition. Belief in God is the outcome of mysticism which is the natural consequence of depression. That this world is *'Maya'* or *'Mithya'*, a dream or a fiction, is clear mysticism which has been originated and developed by Hindu sages of old ages, such as Shankaracharya and others. But in the materialist philosophy, this mode of thinking has got absolutely no place. But this mysticism of the thinking has got absolutely no place. But this mysticism of the author is by no means ignoble or deplorable. It has its own of them are doing very productive labour. The only difference that the socialist society expects is that the mental workers shall no longer be regarded superior to the manual workers.

L. Ram Saran Das's idea about free education is really worth considering, and the socialist government has adopted somewhat the same course in Russia.

His discussion about crime is really the most advanced school of thought. Crime is the most serious social problem which needs a very tactful treatment. He has been in jail for the better part of his life. He has got the practical experience. At one place he employs the typical jail terms, 'the light labour, the medium labour, and the hard labour', etc. Like all other socialists he suggests that, instead of retribution, i.e., retaliation, the reformative theory should form the basis of punishment. Not to punish but to reclaim should be the guiding principle of the administration of justice. Jails should be reformatories and not veritable hells. In this connection, the readers should study the Russian prison system.

While dealing with militia he discusses war as well. In my opinion, war as an institution shall only occupy a few pages in the Encyclopaedia then, and war materials shall adorn the no conflicting or diverse interests that cause war.

At the utmost we can say that war shall have to be retained as an institution for the transitional period. We can easily understand if we take the example of the present-day Russia. There is the dictatorship of the proletariat at present. They want to establish a socialist society. Meanwhile, they have to maintain an army to defend themselves against the capitalist society. But the war-aims would be different. Imperialist designs shall no more actuate our dreamland people to wage wars. There shall be no more war trophies. The revolutionary armies shall march to other lands not to bring rulers down from their thrones and stop their blood-sucking exploitation and thus to liberate the toiling masses. But, there shall not be the primitive national or racial hatred to goad our men to fight.

World-federation is the most popular and immediate object of all the free-thinking people, and the author has well dilated on the subject, and his criticism of the so-called League of Nations is beautiful.

In a footnote under stanza 571 (572), the author touches, though briefly, the question of methods. He says: "Such a kingdom cannot be brought about by physical violent revolutions. It cannot be forced upon society from without. It must grow from within.... This can be brought about by the gradual process of Evolution, by educating the masses on the lines mentioned above," etc. This statement does not in itself contain any discrepancy. It is quite correct, but having not been fully explained, is liable to create some misunderstanding, or worse still, a confusion. Does it mean that L. Ram Saran Das has realized the futility of the cult of force? Has he become an orthodox believer in non-violence? No, it does not mean that.

Let me explain what the above quoted statement amounts to. The revolutionaries know better than anybody else that the socialist society cannot be brought about by violent means, but that it should grow and evolve from within. The author suggests education as the only weapon to be employed. But, everybody can easily realize that the present government here, or, as a matter of fact, all the capitalist governments are not only not going to help any such effort, but on the contrary, suppress it mercilessly. Then, what will his 'evolution' achieve? We, the revolutionaries, are striving to capture power in our hands and to organize a revolutionary government which should employ all its resources for mass education, as is being done in Russia today. After capturing power, peaceful methods shall be employed for constructive work; force shall be employed to crush the obstacles. If that is what the author means, then we are at one. And I am confident that it is exactly this what he means.

I have discussed the book at great length. I have rather criticized it. But, I am not going to ask any alteration in it, because this has got its historical value. These were the ideas of 1914-15 revolutionaries.

I strongly recommend this book to young men in particular, but with a warning. Please do not read it to follow blindly and take for granted what is written in it. Read it, criticize it, think over it, try to formulate your own ideas with its help.

26

Manifestos of Naujawan Bharat Sabha and Hindustan Socialist Republican Association

The manifestos of Naujawan Bharat Sabha and Hindustan Socialist Republican Association—drafted by Bhagwati Charan Vohra (founder-propaganda secretary of NBS) in consultation with Bhagat Singh—provide great insights into the political ideals of these revolutionaries.

Manifesto of Naujawan Bharat Sabha (NBS), Punjab (April, 1928)

Young Comrades,

Our country is passing through a chaos. There is mutual distrust and despair prevailing everywhere. The great leaders have lost faith in the cause and most of them no more enjoy the confidence of the masses. There is no programme and no enthusiasm among the 'champions' of Indian independence. There is chaos everywhere. But chaos is inevitable and a necessary phase in the course of making of a nation. It is during such critical periods that the sincerity of the workers is tested, their character built, real programme formed, and then, with a new spirit, new, hopes, new faith and enthusiasm, the work is started. Hence, there is nothing to be disgusted of.

We are, however, very fortunate to find ourselves on the threshold of a new era. We no more hear the news of reaching chaos that used to be sung vastly in praise of the British bureaucracy. The historic question "Would you be governed by sword or pen?", no more lies unanswered. Those who put that question to us have themselves answered it. In the words of Lord Birkenhead, "With the sword we won India and with the sword we shall retain it." Thanks to this candour everything is clear now. After remembering Jallianwala and Manawala outrages it looks absurd to quote that "A good government cannot be a substitute for self-government." It is self-evident.

A word about the blessings of the British rule in India. Is it necessary to quote the whole volumes of Romesh Chandra Dutt, William Digby, and Dadabhai Naoroji in evidence to prove the decline and ruin of Indian industries? Does it require any authorities to prove that India, with the richest soil and mine, is today one of the poorest, that India, which could be proud of so glorious a civilizations, is today the most backward country with only 5% literacy? Do not the people know that India has to pay the largest toll of human life with the highest child death rate in the world? The epidemics like plague, cholera, influenza, and such other diseases are becoming common day by day. Is it not disgraceful for us to hear again and again that we are not fit for self-government? Is it not really degrading for us, with Guru Govind Singh, Shivaji, and Hari Singh as our heroes; to be told that we are incapable of defending ourselves? Alas, we have done little to prove the contrary. Did we not see our trade and commerce being crushed in its very infancy in the first effort of Guru Nanak steamship co-started by Baba Gurdit Singh in 1914; the inhuman treatment meted out to them, far away in Canada, on the way, and finally, the bloody reception of those despairing, broken-hearted passengers with valleys of shots at Bajbaj, and what not? Did we not see all this? In India, where for the honour of one Dropadi, the great Mahabharat was fought, dozens of them were ravaged in 1919. They were spit at, in their naked faces. Did we not see all this? Yet, we are content with the existing order of affairs. Is this life worth living?

Does it require any revelation now to make us realize that we are enslaved and must be free? Shall we wait for an uncertain sage to make us feel that we are an oppressed people? Shall we expectantly wait for divine help or some miracle to deliver us from bondage? Do we not know the fundamental principles of liberty? "Those who want to be free, must themselves strike the blow." Young men, awake, arise; we have slept too long!

We have appealed to the young only. Because the young bear the most inhuman tortures smilingly and face death without hesitation. Because the whole history of human progress is written with the blood of young men and young women. And because the reforms are ever made by the vigour, courage, self-sacrifice and emotional conviction of the young men who do not know enough to be afraid and who feel much more than they think.

Were it not the young men of Japan who come forth in hundreds to throw themselves in the ditches to make a dry path to Port Arthur? And Japan is today one of the foremost nations in the world. Were it not the young Polish people who fought again and again and failed, but fought again heroically throughout the last century? And today we see a free Poland. Who freed Italy from the Austrian yoke? Young Italy.

Do you know the wonders worked by the Young Turks? Do you not daily read what the young Chinese are doing?

Were it not the young Russians who scarified their lives for Russians emancipation? Throughout the last century hundreds and thousands of them were exiled to Siberia for the mere distribution of socialist pamphlets or, like Dostoyevsky, for merely belonging to socialist debating society. Again and again they faced the storm of oppression. But they did not lose the courage. It were they, the young only, who fought. And everywhere the young can fight without hope, without fear and without hesitation. And we find today in the great Russia, the emancipation of the world.

While, we Indians, what are we doing? A branch of peepal tree is cut and religious feelings of the Hindus are injured. A corner of a paper idol, tazia, of the idol-breaker Mohammedans is broken, and 'Allah' gets enraged, who cannot be satisfied with anything less than the blood of the infidel Hindus. Man ought to be attached more importance that the animals and, yet, here in India, they break each other's heads in the name of 'sacred animals'. Our vision is circumscribed by....

There are many others among us who hide their lethargy under the garb of internationalism. Asked to serve their country they reply: "Oh Sirs, we are cosmopolitans and believe in universal brotherhood. Let us not quarrel with the British. They are our brothers." A good idea, a beautiful phrase. But they miss its implication. The doctrine of universal brotherhood demands that the exploitation of man by man and nation by nation must be rendered impossible. Equal opportunity to all without any sort of distinction. But British rule in India is a direct negation of all these, and we shall have nothing to do with it.

A word about social servicre here. Many good men think that social service (in the narrow sense, as it is used and understood in our country) is the panacea to all our ills and the best method of serving the country. Thus, we find many ardent youth contending themselves with distributing grain among the poor and nursing the sick all their life. These men are noble and self-denying but they cannot understand that charity cannot solve the problem of hunger and disease in India and, for that matter, in any other country.

Religious superstitions and bigotry are a great hinderance in our progress. They have proved to be an obstacle in our way and we must do away with them. "The thing that cannot bear free thought must perish." There are many other such weakness which we are to overcome. The conservativeness and orthodoxy of the Hindus, extra-territorialism and fanaticism of the Mohammedans and narrow-mindedness of all the communities, in general, are always exploited by the foreign enemy. Young men with revolutionary zeal from all communities are required for the task.

Having achieved nothing, we are not prepared to sacrifice anything for any achievement; our leaders are fighting amongst themselves to decide what will be the share of each community in the hoped achievement. Simply to conceal their cowardice and lack of spirit of self-sacrifice, they are creating a false issue and screening the real one. These arm-chair politicians have their eyes set on the handful of bones that may be thrown to them, as they hope, by the mighty rulers. That is extremely humiliating. Those who come forth to fight the battle of liberty cannot sit and decide first that after so much sacrifices, so much achievement must be sure and so much share to be divided. Such people never make any sort of sacrifice. We want people who may be prepared to fight without hope, without fear, and without hesitation, and who may be willing to die unhonoured, unwept, and unsung. Without that spirit, we will not be able to fight the great two-fold battle that lies before us—two-fold because of the internal foe, on the one hand, and a foreign enemy, on the other. Our real battle is against our own disabilities which are exploited by the enemy and some of our own people for their selfish motives.

Young Punjabis, the youth of other provinces are working tremendously in their respective spheres. The organization and awakening displayed by young Bengal on February 3, should serve as an example to us. Our Punjab, despite the greatest amount of sacrifice and suffering to its credit, is described as a politically-backward province. Why? Because, although it belongs to the martial race, we are lacking in organization and discipline; we who are proud of the ancient University of Texila, today, stand badly in need of culture. And a culture requires fine literature which cannot be prepared without a common and well-developed language. Alas, we have got none.

While trying to solve the above problem that faces our country, we will also have to prepare the masses to fight the greater battle that lies before us. Our political struggle began just after the great War of Independence of 1857. It has passed through different phases. Along with the advent of the twentieth century, the British bureaucracy has adopted quite a new policy towards India. They are drawing our bourgeoisie and petty bourgeoisie into their fold by adopting the policy of concessions. Their cause is being made common. The progressive investment of British capital in India will inevitably lead to that end. In the very near future, we will find that class and their great leaders having thrown their lot with the foreign rulers. Some round-table conference or any such body will end in a compromise between the two. They will no more be lions and cubs. Even without any conciliation the expected Great War of the entire people will surely thin the ranks of the so-called champions of India independence.

The future programme of preparing the country will begin with the motto: "Revolution by the masses and for the masses." In other words, Swaraj for the 90%; Swaraj not only attained by the masses but also for the masses. This is a very difficult task. Though our leaders have offered many suggestions, none had the courage to put forward and carry out successfully and concrete scheme of awakening the masses. Without going into details, we can safely assert that to achieve our object, thousands of our most brilliant young men, like Russian youth, will have to pass their precious lives in village and make people understand what the Indian revolution would really mean. They must be made to realize that the revolution which is to come will mean more than a change of masters. It will, above all, mean the birth of new order of things, a new state. This is not the work of a day or a year. Decades of matchless self-sacrifice will prepare the masses for the accomplishment of that great work and only the revolutionary young men will be able to do that. A revolutionary does not necessarily mean a man of bombs and revolvers.

The task before the young is hard and their resources are scanty. A great many obstacles are likely to block their way. But the earnestness of the few but sincere can overcome them all. The young must come forth. They must see the hard and difficult path that lies before them, the great tasks they have to perform. They must remember in the heart of hearts that "success is but a chance; sacrifice, a law". Their lives might be the lives of constant failures, even more wretched than those which Guru Govind Singh had to face throughout his life. Even then they must not repent and say, "Oh, it was all an illusion."

Young men, do not get disheartened when you find such a great battle to fight single-handed, with none to help you. You must realize your own latent strength. Rely on yourselves and success is yours. Remember the words of the great mother of James Garfield which she spoke to her son while sending him away, penniless, helpless, and resourceless, to seek his fortune: "Nine times out of ten the best thing that can happen to a young man is to be thrown overboard to swim or sink for himself." Glory to the mother who said these words and glory to those who will rely on them.

Mazzini, that oracle of Italian regeneration, once said: "All great national movements begin with unknown men of the people without influence, except for the faith and the will that counts neither time nor difficulties." Let the boat of life weigh another time. Let it set sail in the Great Ocean, and then:

> *Anchor is in no stagnant shallow.*
> *Trust the wide and wonderous sea,*
> *Where the tides are fresh for ever,*
> *And the mighty currents free.*
> *There perchance, O young Columbus,*
> *Your new world of truth may be.*

Do not hesitate, let not the theory of incarnation haunt your mind and break your courage. Everybody can become great if he strives. Do not forget your own martyrs. Kartar Singh was a young man. Yet, in this teens, when he came forth to serve his country, he ascended the scaffold smiling and echoing *"Bande Mataram"*. Bhai Balmukund and Awadh Bihari were both quite young when they gave their lives for the cause. They were from amongst you. You must try to become as sincere patriots and as ardent lovers of liberty as they were. Do not lose patience and sense at one time, and hope at another. Try to make stability and determination a second nature to yourselves.

Let young men think independently, calmly, serenely, and patiently. Let them adopt the cause of Indian independence as the sole aim of their lives. Let them stand on their own feet. They must organize themselves free from any influence and refuse to be exploited any more by the hypocrites and insincere people who have nothing in common with them and who always desert the cause at the critical juncture. In all seriousness and sincerity, let them make the triple motto of "service, suffering, sacrifice" their sole guide. Let them remember that "the making of a nation requires self-sacrifice of thousands of obscure men and women who care more for the idea of their country than for their own comfort and interest, than own lives and the lives of those who they love".

Manifesto of the Hindustan Socialist Republican Association (HSRA) (1929)

"The food on which the tender plant of liberty thrives is the blood of the martyr."

For decades, this life blood to the plant of India's liberty is being supplied by revolutionaries. There are a few to question the magnanimity of the noble ideals they cherish and the grand sacrifices they have offered, but their normal activities being mostly secret, the country is in dark as to their present policy and intentions. This has necessitated the Hindustan Socialist Republican Association to issue this manifesto.

This association stands for revolution in India in order to liberate her from foreign domination by means of organized armed rebellion. Open rebellion by a subject people must always in the nature of things be preceded by secret propaganda and secret propaganda and secret preparations. Open rebellion by a subject people must always in the nature of things be preceded by secret propaganda and secret preparations. Once a country enters that phase the task of an alien government becomes impossible. It might linger on for a number of years, but its fate is sealed. Human nature, with all its prejudices and conservatism, has a sort of instinctive dread for revolution. Upheavals have always been a terror to holders of power and privilege. Revolution is a phenomenon which nature loves and without which there can be no progress either in nature or in human affairs. Revolution is certainly not unthinking, a brutal campaign of murder and incendiarism; it is not a few bombs thrown here and a few shots fired there; neither is it a movement to destroy all ramnants of civilization and blow to pieces time-honoured principles of justice and equity. Revolution is not a philosophy of despair or a creed of desperadoes. Revolution may be anti-God, but is certainly not anti-Man. It is a vital, living force which is indicative of eternal conflict between the old and the new, between life and living death, between life and living death, between light and darkness. There is no concord, no symphony, no rhythm without revolution. 'The music of the spheres' of which poets have sung, would remain an unreality if a ceaseless revolution were to be eliminated from the space. Revolution is Law, Revolution is Order, and Revolution is the Truth.

The youths of our nation have realized this truth. They have learnt painfully the lesson that without revolution there is no possibility of enthroning order, law, and love in place of chaos and legal vandalism and hatred which are reigning supreme today. Let no one, in this blessed land of ours, run with the idea that the youths are irresponsible. They know where they stand. None knows better than their own selves, that their path is not strewn with roses. Form time to time, they have paid a fairly decent price for their ideals. It does not, therefore, lie in the mouth of anybody to say that youthful impetuosity has feasted upon platitudes. It is no good to hurl denunciatory epithets at our ideology. It is enough to know that our ideas are sufficiently active and powerful to drive us on aye even to gallows.

It has become a fashion these days to indulge in wild and meaningless talk of non-violence. Mahatma Gandhi is great and we mean no disrespect to him if we express our emphatic disapproval of the methods advocated by him for our country's emancipation. We would be ungrateful to him if we do not salute him for the immense awakening that has been brought about by his non-cooperation movement in the country. But to us, the Mahatma is an impossible visionary. Non-violence may be a noble ideal, but is a thing of the morrow. We can, situated as we are, never hope to win our freedom by mere non-violence. The world is armed to the very teeth. And the world is too much with us. All talk of peace may be sincere, but such false ideology. What logic, we ask, is there in asking the country to traverse a non-violent path when the world atmosphere is surcharged with violence and exploitation of the weak? We declare with all the emphasis we can command that the youths of the nation cannot be lured by such midsummer night's dreams.

We believe in violence, not as an end itself but as a means to a noble end. And the votaries of non-violence, as also the advocates of caution and circumspection, will readily grant this much at least that we know how to suffer for and to act up to our convictions. Shall we here recount all those sacrifices which our comrades have offered at the altar of our common Mother? Many a heartrending and soul-stirring scene has been enacted inside the four walls of His Majesty's prison. We have been taken to task for our terroristic policy. Our answer is that terrorism is never the object of revolutionaries, nor do they believe that terrorism alone can bring independence. No doubt the revolutionaries think, and rightly, that it is only by resorting to terrorism alone that they can find a most effective means of retaliation. The British government exists, because the Britishers have been successful in terrorising the whole of India. How are we to meet this official terrorism? Only counter-terrorism on the part of revolutionaries can checkmate effectively this bureaucratic bullying. A feeling of utter helplessness pervades society. How can we overcome this fatal despondency? It is only by infusing a real spirit of sacrifice that lost self-confidence can be restored. Terrorism has its international aspect also. England's enemies, which are many, are drawn towards us by effective demonstration of our strength. That, in itself, is a great advantage.

Indian is writhing under the yoke of imperialism. Her teeming millions are today a helpless prey to poverty and ignorance. Foreign domination and economic exploitation have unmanned the vast majority of the people who constitute the workers and peasants of India. The position of the Indian proletariat is, today, extremely critical. It has a double danger to face. It has to bear to onslaught of foreign capital on the other. The latter is showing a progressive tendency to join forces with the former. The leaning of certain politicians in favour of dominion status shows clearly which way the wind blows. Indian capital is preparing to betray the masses into the hands of foreign capitalism and receive as a price of this betrayal, a little share in the government of the country. The hope of the proletariat is, therefore, now centred on socialism which alone can lead to the establishment of complete independence and the removal of all social distinction and privileges.

The future of India rests with the youths. They are the salt of the earth. Their promptness to suffer, their daring courage, and their radiant sacrifice prove that India's future in their hands is perfectly safe. In a moment of realization, the late Deshbandhu Das said: "The youths are at once the hope and glory of the Motherland. Theirs is the inspiration behind the movement. Theirs is the sacrifice. Theirs is the victory. They are torch bearers on the road to freedom. They are the pilgrims on the road to liberty."

Youths, ye soldiers of the Indian Republic, fall in: do not stand easy, do not let your knees tremble. Shake off the paralyzing effects of long lethargy. Yours is a noble mission. Go out into every nook and corner of the country and prepare the ground for future revolution which is sure to come. Respond to the clarion call of duty. Do not [be a] vegetable. Grow! Every minute of your life you must think of devising means so that this ancient land may arise with flaming eyes and fierce yawn. Sow the seeds of disgust and hatred against British imperialism in the fertile minds of your fellow youths. And the seeds shall sprout and there shall grow a jungle of sturdy trees, because you shall water the seeds with your warm blood. Then a grim and terrible earthquake having a universally destructive potentiality shall inevitably come along with portentous rumblings, and this edifice of imperialism will crash and crumble to dust, and great shall be the fall therefore. And then, and not till then, a new Indian nation shall arise and surprise humanity with the splendour and glory, all its own. The wise and the mighty shall be bewildered by the simple and the weak.

Individual liberty shall be safe. The sovereignty of the proletariat shall be recognized. We court the advent of such revolution. Long Live Revolution!

Kartar Singh,
President

Sources

Most of the letters and statements have been sourced from ShahidBhagatSingh.Org, (organization founded by Prof. Jagmohan Singh, nephew of Bhagat Singh), and Marxist Internet Archive. Some of the essays have been sourced from *Shahid Bhagat Singh Dastavejo Ke Aaine Main*, (a Hindi collection of essays edited by Dr. Chaman Lal and published by Publications Division, Ministry of Information and Broadcasting, Government of India). These essays have been translated by Dr. Hina Nandrajog, Officiating Principal of the Vivekananda College, University of Delhi.

1. **"My Life Has Been Dedicated to the Cause of Azad-E-Hind" A 16-Year-Old Bhagat Singh Wrote to His Father (1923) (Originally in Hindi)**
   Marxist Internet Archive
   https://www.marxists.org/hindi/bhagat-singh/1923/ghar-ko-alvida.htm

2. **"Blood Sprinkled on the Day of Holi, Babbar Akalis on the Crucifix!" Bhagat Singh on Martyrs of Babbar Akali Movement (March, 1926)**
   Source: Shahidbhagatsingh.org
   https://www.shahidbhagatsingh.org/index.asp?link=day_of_holi

3. **The Religious Riots and Their Solution (June, 1927)**
   Shahid Bhagat Singh Dastavejo Ke Aaine Main; Edited by Dr. Chaman Lal (A Hindi collection of essays published by Publications Division, Ministry of Information and Broadcasting, Government of India). Essay translated by Dr. Nina Nandrajog.

4. **Religion and Our Freedom Struggle (May, 1928)**
   Shahid Bhagat Singh Dastavejo Ke Aaine Main; Edited by Dr. Chaman Lal (A Hindi collection of essays published by Publications Division, Ministry of Information and Broadcasting, Government of India). Essay translated by Dr. Nina Nandrajog.

5. **The Issue of Untouchability (June, 1928)**
   Shahid Bhagat Singh Dastavejo Ke Aaine Main; Edited by Dr. Chaman Lal (A Hindi collection of essays published by Publications Division, Ministry of Information and Broadcasting, Government of India). Essay translated by Dr. Nina Nandrajog.

6. **Satyagraha and Strikes (June, 1928)**
   Shahid Bhagat Singh Dastavejo Ke Aaine Main; Edited by Dr. Chaman Lal (A Hindi collection of essays published by Publications Division, Ministry of Information and Broadcasting, Government of India). Essay translated by Dr. Nina Nandrajog.

7. **Students and Politics (July, 1928)**
   Source: *Shahid Bhagat Singh Dastavejo Ke Aaine Main*; Edited by Dr. Chaman Lal (A Hindi collection of essays published by Publications Division, Ministry of Information and Broadcasting, Government of India). Essay translated by Dr. Nina Nandrajog.

8. **New Leaders and Their Different Ideas (July, 1928)**
   Shahid Bhagat Singh Dastavejo Ke Aaine Main; Edited by Dr. Chaman Lal (A Hindi collection of essays published by Publications Division, Ministry of Information and Broadcasting, Government of India). Essay translated by Dr. Nina Nandrajog.

9. **What Is Anarchism - I, II, and III (July, 1928)**
   Shahid Bhagat Singh Dastavejo Ke Aaine Main; Edited by Dr. Chaman Lal (A Hindi collection of essays published by Publications Division, Ministry of Information and Broadcasting, Government of India). Essay translated by Dr. Nina Nandrajog.

10. **"Beware, Ye Tyrants; Beware" (December, 1928)**
    ShahidBhagatSingh.Org
    https://www.shahidbhagatsingh.org/index.asp?link=republican_army

11. **"It Takes a Loud Voice to Make the Deaf Hear!" (April, 1929)**
    ShahidBhagatSingh.Org
    https://www.shahidbhagatsingh.org/index.asp?link=april8

12. **"Do Away with the Fear of Doing Radical Things" Bhagat Singh Wrote to Shaheed Sukhdev (April, 1929)**
    ShahidBhagatSingh.Org
    https://www.shahidbhagatsingh.org/index.asp?link=april5

13. **Joint Statement: Full Text of Statement of Bhagat Singh and B.K. Dutt regarding the Assembly Bomb Case (June, 1929)**
    ShahidBhagatSingh.Org
    https://www.shahidbhagatsingh.org/index.asp?link=june6

14. **Hunger-Strikers' Demand (June, 1929)**
    ShahidBhagatSingh.Org
    https://www.shahidbhagatsingh.org/hunger_strike.asp

15. **Message to Punjab Students' Conference (October, 1929)**
    ShahidBhagatSingh.Org
    https://www.shahidbhagatsingh.org/index.asp?link=student_conference

16. **On the Slogan of 'Long Live Revolution!' (December, 1929)**
    ShahidBhagatSingh.Org
    https://www.shahidbhagatsingh.org/index.asp?link=dec24

17. **Why I Am an Atheist (October, 1930)**
    ShahidBhagatSingh.Org
    https://www.shahidbhagatsingh.org/index.asp?link=atheist

18. **"Show the World That the Revolutionaries Not Only Die For Their Ideals but Can Face Every Calamity!" Bhagat Singh Wrote to B. K. Dutt (November, 1930)**
    ShahidBhagatSingh.Org
    https://www.shahidbhagatsingh.org/index.asp?link=letter_bkdutt

19. **"I Want to Tell You That Obstacles Make a Man Perfect" Bhagat Singh Wrote to Sukhdev on Suicide (1930)**
    ShahidBhagatSingh.Org
    https://www.shahidbhagatsingh.org/index.asp?link=regarding_suicide

20. **Hunger-Strikers' Demands Reiterated (January 28, 1930)**
    ShahidBhagatSingh.Org
    https://www.shahidbhagatsingh.org/index.asp?link=hunger_strike_demands

21. **"I Feel as Though I Have Been Stabbed in the Back" Bhagat Singh Wrote to His Father from Jail (October, 1930)**
    Marxist Internet Archive
    https://www.marxists.org/archive/bhagat-singh/1930/10/04.htm

22. **To Young Political Workers (February, 1931)**
    ShahidBhagatSingh.Org
    https://www.shahidbhagatsingh.org/index.asp?link=political_workers

23. "We Are War Prisoners, Shoot Us, Do Not Hang Us!" Bhagat Singh's Last Petition Letter to the Governor of Punjab, Shimla (March, 1931)
    ShahidBhagatSingh.Org
    https://www.shahidbhagatsingh.org/index.asp?link=bhagat_petition

24. "Mr. Kishan's Action Was Part of the Struggle Itself" Bhagat Singh Regarding Line of Defence in Hari Kishan's Case (June, 1931)
    ShahidBhagatSingh.Org
    https://www.shahidbhagatsingh.org/index.asp?link=hari_kishan_case

25. Introduction to Dreamland (not known)
    ShahidBhagatSingh.Org
    https://www.shahidbhagatsingh.org/index.asp?link=dreamland

26. Manifestos of Naujawan Bharat Sabha (NBS), Punjab (April, 1928) and Hindustan Socialist Republican Association (HSRA) (1929)
    ShahidBhagatSingh.Org
    http://www.shahidbhagatsingh.org/index.asp?link=bharat_sabha

Milton Keynes UK
Ingram Content Group UK Ltd.
UKHW020935110624
444053UK00015B/922